How to Live a Prosperous Life

Discover the Keys to Abundance

How to Live a Prosperous Life

Catherine Ponder
Author of *The Dynamic Laws of Prosperity*

Published 2024 by Gildan Media LLC
aka G&D Media
www.GandDmedia.com

How to Live a Prosperous Life was published by the Unity School of Christianity, Lee's Summit, Missouri, 1962.

First G&D Media edition 2024.

No part of this book may be used, reproduced or transmitted in any manner whatsoever, by any means (electronic, photocopying, recording, or otherwise), without the prior written permission of the author, except in the case of brief quotations embodied in critical articles and reviews. No liability is assumed with respect to the use of the information contained within. Although every precaution has been taken, the author and publisher assume no liability for errors or omissions. Neither is any liability assumed for damages resulting from the use of the information contained herein.

Front cover design by David Rheinhardt of Pyrographx

Interior design by Meghan Day Healey of Story Horse, LLC.

Library of Congress Cataloging-in-Publication Data is available upon request

ISBN: 978-1-7225-0686-5

10 9 8 7 6 5 4 3 2 1

Contents

Chapter 1
    Dare to Prosper!......................7

Chapter 2
    Pray and Prosper.....................27

Chapter 3
    Making the Right
    Contact for Prosperity................47

Chapter 4
    Substance—the Key to Prosperity......57

Chapter 5
    The Prosperity Law of Increase........69

Chapter 6
    Tithe Your Way to Prosperity 77

Chapter 7
    There Is Magic in It 89

Chapter 8
    Wheel of Fortune.....................93

Chapter 9
    Harvest Your Good 99

Chapter 10
    Prosperity, the Hope of the World 107

Chapter 11
    What You Can Do
    about World Peace.................. 115

Chapter 12
    Prosperous Thinking for Health 129

Chapter 13
    Controlled Living................... 145

Chapter 14
    A Master Plan for Success 153

CHAPTER 1

Dare to Prosper!

Prosperity comes not by chance but in accordance with absolute law. Charles Fillmore has said: "The law of supply is a divine law. This means that it is a law of mind and must work through mind." In other words, the peace, health, and plenty of prosperity must come through prosperous thinking. The mind can be trained to think prosperously in simple, delightful ways, and the results of prosperous thinking are also delightful, practical, and satisfying.

A businessman had had a serious heart condition most of his life. As he began to practice prosperous thinking, he relaxed more and more in mind, body, and affairs. As he began to make his mind work for him in prosperous, healthy, victorious ways, tension disappeared; and after a time his physician stated that the heart condition had been healed. Today this man enjoys the best health of his life.

A lonely, unhappy career woman, who had often threatened suicide, learned about prosperous thinking, and became so fascinated with its practical power that she found new interests outside herself. She developed a new lease on life. The suicide talk stopped, and today she is a transformed individual.

A businessman who drank secretly found that as he began invoking prosperous thinking, he was able to resolve and dissolve inner hostilities and conflicts, through new, victorious attitudes. His desire to drink vanished.

In several instances, a marriage was saved after one of the partners learned of and began quietly to practice prosperous thinking. A widow who had been alone for twenty years met and married happily. One person's divorced partner returned, and they were remarried.

A businessman who had always detested his work discovered that as he applied prosperous thinking to his job, he got a whole new perspective on it. In due time, this man was sought out by many for counseling. Needless to say, he no longer considers his work detestable, and he enjoys the many contacts he has with others.

What were the simple but delightful steps these persons and many others took to invoke prosperous thinking, thus producing peace, health, and plenty in their lives?

First, they got ready for the prosperity they desired by creating a vacuum to receive it. Nature abhors a vacuum and always rushes in with new substance to fill empty space, in mind, body, affairs, or relationships.

You too can form a mental vacuum by cleaning out of your mind negative, limited, unforgiving thoughts. As Charles Fillmore has written, "Thoughts are things and occupy 'space' in mind. We cannot have new or better ones in a place already crowded with old, weak, inefficient thoughts. A mental housecleaning is even more necessary than a material one." If you are not sure what attitudes or memories need to be released and dissolved, give yourself a universal treatment in release and forgiveness. Declare:

"I fully and freely forgive. I loose and let go. I cast all judgments, resentments, criticism, and unforgiveness upon the Christ within, to be dissolved and

healed. The prospering Truth has set me free to meet my rich good and to share my good with others."

As you prayerfully affirm this, you will probably feel a sense of burden pass and a feeling of release, relief, and freedom come. Your mental vacuum for new good has now been formed.

A businessman became ill, and in spite of the best medical care he did not recover. His body was filled with poison and nothing seemed to dissolve it. One night while perspiring with a high fever, this man realized that there must be something he needed to get rid of or release, mentally or emotionally, since thoughts and emotions have such a powerful effect on the body. He then asked God to reveal what it was that he needed to release.

Suddenly he began to think of a person against whom he had been holding a strong grudge and about whom he had said many unkind things. He then affirmed over and over: *"I fully and freely release and forgive. I loose and let go all ill feeling. Divine love produces the perfect result now."* Soon a feeling of peace, quietness, and release came, and he slept peacefully. The next morning his fever was gone and he recovered rapidly from his illness of many months' duration.

Not only is it necessary to form a mental vacuum; often a physical vacuum must be formed. You can form a physical vacuum for new peace, health, and plenty by releasing, giving away, selling or otherwise getting rid of what you no longer want or need. Do not retain items of clothing, furniture, letters, files, books, or any other personal possessions that you no longer need or use. Get them out of the way to make room for what you do want. As long as you retain them, they take up space in your world that is needed for your new good. Declare to yourself as you go through your personal belongings: *"I fully and freely release. I loose and let go. I joyously make way for my new good, which now appears quickly in satisfying, appropriate form."*

A widow had attempted in vain to settle her late husband's estate. Many legal entanglements had involved her with other heirs for almost a year. When she learned about forming a vacuum, she began cleaning out closets and other areas of her husband's clothes and personal possessions. The estate was quickly and harmoniously settled. A widower, whose grief for his deceased wife had been intense for several years, found that as he freely and fully released her personal possessions his grief lessened and he was able to begin building a new life for himself. A husband had asked his wife for a divorce and they were separated; then she learned of the vacuum law of prosperity. After she sold or otherwise disposed of a great many personal possessions left over from a former marriage, her present husband returned and they were happily reconciled.

Sometimes it is necessary to form a vacuum by letting go of unsatisfying relationships and old ways of living that no longer please or satisfy. A woman who had had great financial needs found that new ideas and methods of work opened to her, after she gave up several dissatisfying friends of the past with whom she was no longer congenial. If there is a question in your mind about this possibility, affirm: *"I now let go old ways of living, old, unsatisfactory methods of work, and dissatisfying relationships of the past. I am now open and receptive to my new and highest good."*

You are now ready to take the second step in prosperous thinking. Charles Fillmore described this step when he wrote: "Go into the silence daily at a stated time and concentrate on the substance of Spirit prepared for you from the foundation of the world. This opens up a current of thought that will bring prosperity into your affairs." Daily become still, and think about the rich, unlimited substance of the universe that is everywhere present for you to form as prosperous ideas, which will produce prosperous results. Affirm: *"The rich substance of the universe instantly responds to my prosperous thinking. I am now rich in mind and manifestation."* At this point begin definitely to mold substance. Do this by sitting quietly every day and writing down on paper what you feel you want to be, have, accomplish, and experience for the day, week, month, or year.

Dare to be definite about prosperity, if you want prosperity to be definite in manifesting for you. People often hesitate to write down and think about what they really desire. They do not realize that the mind is the connecting link between man and the rich but unformed substance of the universe. If you never think definitely about the prosperous results you desire, no mental contact is made with the rich substance of the universe; you must drift along in a stream of limitation and dissatisfaction.

A businesswoman attended a lecture on prosperous thinking and learned of the power of writing down her desires. She hurried home and made a list of the prosperous results she strongly desired in her life. Four days later a large sum of money, to which she had long been legally entitled but had been unable to collect, came to her.

The rich substance of the universe is yours to do with as you wish. Why settle for so little in life when you can have so much, just by daring to be definite in your thinking? Another businesswoman, a widow, began writing out her true desires daily, at the first of a new year. She wrote down her desire to remarry happily. She wrote down her desire for a better home. She also stipulated her deep desire for a better paying, more satisfying job. In the middle of the year, a pleasant, better-paying position was offered to her. At about the same time, she met her future husband, through mutual friends. They were married by the end of the year. He was a building contractor, and he gave her the better home she wanted. As he too began deliberately to practice prosperous thinking, he developed two other successful businesses.

When you write down your desires for the day, week, or month, list what you really want—not what you think you should have, nor what somebody else thinks you should have. Your deep-seated desires are God's good tapping at the door of your mind. Furthermore, write down dates by which you wish your desired good to be accomplished. You will be amazed at how the substance of heaven and earth will hasten to do your bidding when you give it definite desires and dates through which to work out good results.

A businessman had long desired larger and better business property, for the expansion of his business. After learning of the power of prosperous thinking, he no longer hesitated to believe he could have the property; instead, he wrote down his definite desires for it. Soon he learned of a desirable piece of business property, and upon investigation found that it was priced quite reasonably. Everyone involved—his lawyer, the realtor, and the seller—tried to assist him in every way. Even the local bank president seemed interested in helping him acquire the property. It was as though all the forces of heaven and earth willingly co-operated to work out the financial arrangements, and this man soon settled his business in the new location.

As you get your desires down on paper, feel free to work and rework them, changing, revising, expanding, and rearranging them as you wish from day to day. Make lists of what you do not want in your life, and write down, concerning them, *"Be thou dissolved, in the name of Jesus Christ."* Make lists of what you do want and write down, *"This or something better, Father. Let Thy highest good now manifest. Let the divine result now appear."* By decreeing the divine result, you remain open and receptive to your highest good, which may appear in the form of greater good than you had humanly conceived in your own private desires.

You are now ready to take the third step in prosperous thinking. Begin, at this point, to image your desires as already fulfilled. Mentally live with the picture of fulfillment as you go about your day. Do not try to reason through your mental pictures of fulfillment, or to understand how they are to come about. Just dare to image the fulfilled result as best you can, and then let the rich substance of the universe produce that imaged good in either usual or unusual ways. For your mental images declare often: *"This or something better, Father. Let Thy highest good now manifest. Let the divine result now appear in the divine way."*

A businessman's wife seemed to be a hopeless alcoholic. She was high-tempered, irresponsible, and very difficult to live with. She and her husband were on the brink of divorce when he learned that mental images make the conditions of mind, body, affairs, and relationships. He persistently began imaging his wife as peaceful, harmonious, responsible, easy to live with, and healed of alcoholism. For months he daily dared to image her as whole in mind, body, affairs, and relationships. Gradually she became calmer, more peaceful and harmonious. She then began taking more interest in herself, her husband, and life generally. I recently had lunch with this couple, and it was apparent that they are healthier, happier, and more prosperous than ever before. Furthermore, this woman's healing and resulting transformation are now complete.

Psychologists declare that imagination is one of the mind's strongest powers. The more you dare to image your desired good as a fulfilled result, and the more you dare to live your mental images, the faster the imaging power of the mind will begin producing almost magical results for you. Your mental images make your conditions, but it is up to you to make your mental images of the good you desire. You should image only the highest and best you can conceive, because, "Whatever you image yourself as doing, you can do." (The treasure-map method is powerful, delightful, and helpful in developing the imaging power of the mind to produce prosperous results.)

The fourth step in prosperous thinking is to begin affirming verbally, definitely, and daily the divine manifestation of your desires. As you daily write down your desires and image them as fulfilled, affirm: *"My world is the perfect creation of divine substance. The finished results of divine substance now appear as peace, health, and plenty in my world."* In the beginning the world was created by definite, spoken affirmations, as God declared, "Let there be . . ." You can and should create your world accordingly, because you are created in the image and likeness of God, and you too have the power to form substance through your definite, spoken decrees for good.

An interior decorator had been out of work for several months and was $2,500 in debt. During a summer slack season she heard about the power of prosperous thinking in overcoming financial lack. She began imaging $2,500 in her checking account to pay all debts, and daily affirmed that her world was the perfect creation of divine substance; that the finished results of divine substance were appearing as peace, health, and plenty in her world. Almost immediately, a friend of a former customer telephoned and asked her to consider decorating an entire apartment house. Her estimate, running into thousands of dollars, was accepted; she was given the decorating job, and her commission amounted to $2,500. This proved to be only the first of a number of profitable jobs that have come to her. She is still joyously affirming: *"My world is the perfect creation of divine substance. The finished remits of divine substance now appear as peace, health, and plenty in my world."*

It is good to be systematic in the daily, verbal use of affirmations, by speaking them aloud in privacy for at least five minutes at a time, three times a day. There is increased power in spoken words to produce definite, satisfying, immediate results. Thinking the right thought is powerful, but speaking it forth into the rich substance of the universe in deliberate, definite, verbal form, over and over daily, gathers that rich substance together in definite events and circumstances that produce immediate, satisfying, and definite results. Charles Fillmore has explained: "Substance is first given form in the mind. . . . In laying hold of substance in the mind and bringing it into manifestation we play a most important part. We do it according to our decree."

A little positive assertion and declaration of the good you desire is often all that is needed to turn the tide of events that will produce that good for you, swiftly and easily. How often have you talked about what you did not want, and gotten it? Now dare to speak of what you desire, and begin receiving it. The promise is: Thou shalt also decree a thing, and it shall be established unto thee."

A man and his wife were salaried employees, barely making a living. They learned about affirmations, and began daily affirming a better income. Soon the man, a draftsman, got the idea of designing greeting cards. His greeting cards soon became so well liked that he and his wife left their jobs and went into the greeting-card business full time. Their income has greatly increased, and their greeting cards have become widely known and purchased.

Use definite affirmations for prosperity when you want definite prosperity results. For the purpose of prosperity the ancient Hebrews affirmed "Jehovah-jireh" when they wished to concentrate on substance. This means "'Jehovah will provide,' the mighty One whose presence and power provides, regardless of any opposing circumstance."

A woman who owned some rental apartments began affirming, *"Jehovah-jireh, the Lord now richly provides,"* during a summer off-season period. Almost immediately her realtor rented one of the apartments for the next season, for $1,900. In another instance, a couple were in financial straits when they learned of the ancient Hebrews' prosperity affirmation. As they affirmed, *"Jehovah-jireh, the Lord now richly provides,"* the way opened for them to sell for cash some property that they had previously felt they might have to mortgage heavily. Another couple's mortgage payments were overdue and they feared losing their home; then they learned of the Hebrews' prosperity affirmation and began affirming, *"Jehovah-jireh, the Lord now richly provides."* Neither had been able to find work for several months. Within a few days the husband obtained work and his wife was offered not one but two jobs, both of which offered higher salaries than any she had previously received. They did not lose their home, and began paying off many miscellaneous debts as well.

After beginning to get rid of what you do not want by forming a vacuum; after writing out your desires, imaging and affirming their divine fulfillment, you are ready for the culminating step in prosperous thinking. The time has come to go about your daily activities, acting as though you are already prosperous, doing whatever you can to make it so in your times of work, play, and rest. This you are to do, however, in a very special way: by invoking the thought of success and prosperity with everything you think, say, and do.

Deliberately become a prosperous thinker by beginning to think of yourself and others as successful, prosperous, victorious. Think often of whatever success, prosperity, and victorious good you are already enjoying, and give thanks for it. Declare to yourself often: *"Every day in every way I am growing more prosperous, successful, victorious. I am made for peace, health, and plenty, and I am now experiencing them in ever-increasing degrees of good."* Give others the same thought whenever you think of them. This is a delightful mental process to which your mind will quickly respond. Stop thinking of the failures and mistakes of yourself or others, and start concentrating on every degree of prosperity, success, and good that has been or is now evident. The mind is strengthened and uplifted by, and thrives on thoughts, images, and words of success; whereas it seems to shrivel and be repelled by thoughts, images, and words of failure, limitation, and poverty. The mind delights in helping a prosperous thinker become more prosperous. That is why "nothing succeeds like success." Invoke the law of increased success by affirming: *"My success is big, powerful, and irresistible. Nothing succeeds like success. I now go from success to greater success, in the name of Jesus Christ."*

Speak in terms of your good rather than in terms of apparent problems. Speak in terms of your blessings rather than in terms of your challenges. Emphasize the good in your life, knowing that as you do, it will increase. How often have you used the law of decrease and talked problems, difficulties, failure, limitation, ill health, confusion, inharmony? Now let your every act, tone, look, word express a quiet, confident assurance of success. Also, give yourself the thought of increased good by thinking of yourself as already looking, acting, and living as successfully and prosperously as you truly desire to be. Think of yourself as already wearing the clothes you wish to wear; as already living in a gracious, abundant manner; as already experiencing the health, prosperity, and happiness you so rightly desire. Then speak positively, appreciatively, of every degree of health, prosperity, and happiness you are already experiencing. This will help to multiply your good.

There is just one other thing to remember: You must persist in doing these simple and delightful things step by step, day by day. Perhaps your mind has been steeped in thoughts, images, and words of failure, limitation, problems, and difficulties. If so, it may take a little while to clear your mind of the negative and make way for positive results. It is important that you persevere.

Napoleon Hill has written something that has helped me persist past discouragement to success many times: "Before success comes in any man's life, he is sure to meet with much temporary defeat and, perhaps, some failure. When defeat overtakes a man, the easiest and most logical thing to do is to QUIT. That is exactly what the majority of men do.

"More than five hundred of the most successful men this country has ever known told the author their greatest success came just one step beyond the point at which defeat had overtaken them." So, if discouragement besets you and your deep longings seem in vain, just hang on to the thought: *"Nothing in the world can take the place of persistence and determination. With God's help I now persist into my highest good."* Persevere in this idea!

Truly, the peace, health, and plenty of prosperity come not by chance but in accordance with the laws of prosperous thinking. You can invoke prosperous thinking for simple, practical, delightful results, as so many others have done.

CHAPTER 2

Pray and Prosper

You are prosperous to the degree that you are experiencing peace, health, and plenty in your world. Prayer can help you experience peace, health, and plenty, because prayer is man's steady effort to know God, and God is the source of all man's good. Thus, in prayer man makes common union with God and His infinite goodness.

It is wonderful, too, to realize that prayer is natural to man, and not a strange, mysterious practice. Man has always prayed and always will. In his primitive understanding, man prayed to the sun and stars, to the fire and water, to animals and plants, to images and myths. Later, as the intellect of man evolved, his ideas changed and he conceived of God as a personal deity with sentiments and emotions—a God with human traits, a God man felt had to be appeased by sacrificial offerings and assailed with pleas for favor. Many of the writers of the Old Testament had this concept of God. Still later, mankind began to come out of a primitive and intellectual understanding of God into a spiritual awareness that God is not a hostile being with a split personality of good and evil, but a God of love, the unchanging Principle of supreme good, both within and around mankind. Methods of prayer that have evolved, expanded, and improved now make it easy to pray to and commune with God.

Brother Lawrence, sixteenth-century French lay brother, who believed greatly in the power of prayer, described his method of prayer as "practicing the presence of God." One biographer has written that Brother Lawrence's one single aim was to bring about a conscious personal union between himself and God and that he took the "shortest cut he could find to accomplish it." And what was his short cut to God? Brother Lawrence described it thus: "The time of business does not with me differ from the time of prayer; and in the noise and clutter of my kitchen, while several persons are at the same time calling for different things, I possess God in as great tranquility as if I were upon my knees at the blessed sacrament." At any moment, in the midst of any occupation, under any circumstances, the soul that wants to know God can "practice the presence."

The one who understands the true nature of God as a rich, loving Father soon realizes that the person who truly prays is bound to succeed, because he attunes himself to the richest, most powerful, most successful force in the universe. Jesus knew this when He promised, "All things whatsoever ye shall ask in prayer, believing, ye shall receive." Tennyson knew it when he wrote, "More things are wrought by prayer than this world dreams of!"

Many people have not employed the power of prayer for prosperity and success because they have gotten the erroneous idea that it is wrong to pray for material things. However, as many of the Biblical promises indicate, it is right and proper that we should pray for the things we need. We live in a rich, friendly universe that desires to fulfill our needs; and prayer is but an act of faith that helps open channels for the fulfillment of our needs.

The Bible is filled with examples of prayers and requests for needful things. Abraham prayed for a son; David prayed for his household; Elijah prayed for rain; Ezekiel prayed for the people; Hannah prayed for a son; Jehoshaphat prayed for deliverance; Jeremiah prayed for freedom from a famine; Nehemiah prayed for protection; Solomon prayed for wisdom. On a number of occasions, Jesus prayed definitely for specific things.

Praying for things is not the only form of prayer, but if we first begin to pray by praying for things (as most of us do), we will learn the power of prayer; and we will then doubtless develop our prayer power further.

Basically, there are four types of prayer: general prayer, the prayer of denial, the prayer of affirmation, and the prayer of meditation and silence. At various times it is good to know and use the various types of prayer to meet life's various needs.

General prayer is the act of praying to God as a loving, understanding Father, in your own way. It can be done on your knees, or more comfortably. It can be expressed through words, or silently. You can have a prayer book before you, or you can browse through your Bible, dwell upon favorite passages and promises.

A simple, effective way to begin a general prayer is to take the Lord's Prayer and ponder each line of it silently or aloud. The ancients believed that the Lord's Prayer was all powerful, and they often declared it over and over, from twelve to fifteen times, without stopping. At various times in the past, at the shrine of Lourdes, some of those seeking healing were taught to pray the Lord's Prayer fifteen times, while they entered the waters. From my own experiences, I know that deep spiritual power is contacted, brought alive, and released when one prays the Lord's Prayer over and over, either silently or verbally. I have known a number of instances where "hard conditions" in business affairs, human relations problems, and health conditions were adjusted when one or more persons prayed the Lord's Prayer from twelve to fifteen times daily.

Another powerful way to make contact with spiritual power in general prayer is to take the name *Jehovah* from the Old Testament or the name *Jesus Christ* from the New Testament, and verbally or silently declare the name over and over. A housewife told me that her husband became very successful in business (after a number of previous failures) when she began daily to call upon and dwell upon the name *Jehovah* in her prayer times.

As for the power of calling on the name *Jesus Christ,* Charles Fillmore has written: "The mightiest vibration is set up by speaking of the name *Jesus Christ.* This is the name that is named 'far above all rule, and authority,' the name above all names, holding in itself all power in heaven and in earth. It is the name that has power to mold the universal substance . . . and when spoken it sets forces into activity that bring results. 'Whatsoever ye shall ask of the Father in my name, he may give it to you.' 'If ye shall ask anything in my name, that will I do.'"

An immigrant once related to me how he was released from a concentration camp, where he had been badly treated, after he began daily calling upon the name *Jesus Christ.* A Christian missionary he met in prison suggested that he pray in this way. At the time, he was supposed to be near death from the many beatings he had received, but instead he began to recover. As he continued dwelling upon this name in his prayers, it was as though a mighty power went to work for him. In a short time, he was released, without explanation, from the concentration camp, even though many of his fellow prisoners were still held and mistreated. As he continued dwelling upon the name of Jesus Christ, further events occurred so that he was able to come to America, where he has lived for a number of happy, grateful years.

Another powerful way to pray is simply to declare, as in the Lord's Prayer, "Thy will be done," since God's will for us is always unlimited good. A musician was out of work. The band with which he worked had been asked to go to Florida. Upon arrival, the promised job did not materialize, and all the members of the band were stranded. This man prayed, "Father, let Thy supreme good will be done in this matter." One day he and the other members of the band were at union headquarters, hoping that something would turn up, when their agent telephoned from New York to say he had located a job for them in Texas.

Another form of general prayer is the prayer of release, of letting go and letting God. When one has "done all," it is good to stand in faith through the prayer of release. A woman was in her farm home in a dense forest area, her husband away on a business trip, when a forest fire broke out. The fire raged all around her property; being surrounded, she could not leave. She prayed, "Father, it's up to You to save me, our house and property. There's nothing more I can do." She then affirmed, "*I let go and let God have His perfect way.*" With a feeling of peace, she released the matter and retired for the night. The next morning she awoke early, to find only a few stumps still burning. The fire had burned right up to her property lines, and stopped. It seemed a miracle. Later in the day when the forest ranger arrived, he said: "There is only one explanation for this. You must have been praying."

You may feel that your prayer experiences have not been particularly satisfying or powerful, or that nothing much has ever happened as a result of your prayers. If so, perhaps it is because you need to develop the other three types of prayer, along with general prayer.

The second type is one that all businesspeople should know about, because they can use it so helpfully as they go about their business. It is the prayer of denial. Many people cringe at the word *denial* thinking that its only meaning is restriction or limitation. But the word deny also means "to reject as a false conception." And prayers of denial are for that purpose: to reject as a false conception that which is not satisfying or good in one's life experiences. Many hundreds of years before the time of Jesus, the Egyptians used the power of denial through the sign of the cross, indicating a crossing out or blotting out of apparent evil.

Prayers of denial are your "no" prayers. They help you to refuse to accept things as they are, to dissolve your negative thoughts about them and thus make way for something better. Prayers of denial are expressed in those attitudes of mind that say: "I will not put up with or tolerate this experience as necessary, lasting, or right. I refuse to accept things as they are; I mentally claim my whole good, knowing that even now it is manifesting." How much mankind needs to use prayers of denial! So many people lead a pygmy existence of fear, compromise, and dissatisfaction when they might be living lives of gigantic good, if they only knew how to say no to less than the best.

Usually, prayers of denial should be followed up by prayers of the third type: prayers of affirmation or "yes" attitudes. It is good to follow up thoughts of what you do not want with thoughts of what you do want; to follow up, "No, I will not accept this" with, "Yes, I will accept this or something better."

Jesus said, "Let your speech be, Yea, yea: Nay, nay." Prayers of denial and affirmation are as much attitudes of mind as they are formal methods of prayer. We can express them silently or verbally wherever we are, either as formal prayers or informally, as attitudes of mind. Charles Fillmore has written that "concentrated attention of the mind on an idea of any kind is equal to prayer, and will make available the spiritual principle that is its source in proportion to the intensity and continuity of the mental effort." In other words, our attitudes are forms of prayer.

The prophet Hosea went into more detail to show how to use denial and affirmative prayer power. He advised, "Take with you words, and return unto Jehovah: say unto him, Take away all iniquity, and accept that which is good." In any situation that is dissatisfying we can deny its power by declaring to a loving Father, "Take away all iniquity." We should then follow up with the affirmation, *"I will accept only that which is good."*

To dissolve especially troublesome problems or hard conditions, it is necessary to concentrate fully upon prayers of denial before giving much attention to affirmative prayers. I once knew a very negative, disagreeable, complaining person with whom I had to work. As far as she was concerned, nothing was right in her world or in the world generally. She was in ill health; she was always battling out things with her family; she was not properly appreciated or compensated on her job; life was "a mess." I offered her some literature on successful living. She liked it, she said. Sometime when she felt better, got through fighting with her family, had schemed properly to get a raise, she planned to read it. In the meantime, she did not care to be distracted from her practice of negative thinking.

The prayer of denial I used was: "*There is nothing but God's love and harmony at work here.*" I hoped that she would subconsciously attune herself to these ideas of love and harmony and let them work for her. In a short time she decided to take another job, and left. The secretary who replaced her was one of the most joyous, harmonious people I have ever met, and delightful to work with. Thus, love and harmony appeared when all else was denied.

So many persons get the erroneous idea that somebody else can keep their good from them; they go through life thinking this. Prayers of denial can dissolve this false belief and the lack that it causes. Declare: "*I dissolve in my own mind, and in the minds of all others, any idea that my own good can be withheld from me. That which is for my highest good now comes to me through God's grace, and I welcome it.*" This prayer of denial can also clear up old conditions of the past, where one's good seemed to have been taken away or withheld.

Another prayer of denial that is helpful when there seem to be barriers or obstacles on your pathway is: "*All barriers and obstacles to my divinely given good are now dissolved, with God's help.*" After using this statement for a time, you will find that whereas before, people, situations, and conditions seemed to work against you, everything will shift; everything will begin working for you. Still another powerful prayer of denial for clearing away negation is: "*The power of God is working through me to free me from every negative influence. Nothing can hold me in bondage. All power is given unto me for good in mind, body, and affairs, and I rightly use it here and now.*"

If people only knew to say no to unhappy experiences, rather than to bow down to them! The Hebrews were warned not to bow down to or worship false idols or gods. The gods of unhappiness, dissatisfaction and limitation are among the major heathen gods of today. To dissolve their appearance in your life, declare often: *"There is nothing for me to fear, God's Spirit of good is at work and divine results are now coming forth."*

When you use denials you erase, dissolve, unform. You should then make firm, new good, through affirmation—the third type of prayer. A traveling salesman who was heavily in debt attempted to get a loan from a bank to pay off his debts. Because he lacked adequate collateral, he was not able to get the loan. He began to affirm: *"God prospers me now."* Within a few days he made a large sale and was able to pay off all his debts, with ample money left over. A businesswoman who was greatly depressed went to a mental hospital for treatment. While doctors were still taking tests to determine the proper treatment, a relative began to affirm daily: *"Perfect love casts out fear and depression."* Within a short time, this woman's depression had dissolved, and she was released and went back to work.

Several years ago a retired sea captain told me that he was healed of alcoholism after he began using the power of affirmation. He affirmed daily: *"I am being healed, with God's help.*" After a time, he began affirming, "*Praise God, I am healed.*" (His whole series of affirmative prayers, which produced a perfect healing, can be found in the Unity pamphlet *A Healing Meditation for Alcoholics.*)

The fourth type of prayer is that of meditation and the silence. It is often in silent, contemplative prayer that we feel the presence of God's goodness most strongly. In this form of prayer, we take a few prayerful words and think about them, silently. As we think about them, they grow in our minds as expanded ideas, moving us to a feeling of peaceful assurance and right ideas (and perhaps later, to right action). If nothing seems to happen in meditation, we have nevertheless made our minds receptive to God's good, which may manifest later.

The Psalmist knew the power of the prayer of meditation and silence when he declared, "Be still and know that I am God." A businessman recently stated that a restless, sleepless night turned into restful sleep after he began meditating upon the Psalmist's words. Dr. Alexis Carrel has described the power of meditation: "When our activity is set toward a precise end, our mental and organic functions become completely harmonized. The unification of the desires, the application of the mind to a single purpose, produce a sort of inner peace. Man integrates himself by meditation, just as by action."

Jesus was constantly going "up into the mountain to pray." After much activity, He often retreated for a time of silent prayer and meditation, to reintegrate Himself. The prophet Haggai pointed out the power of prayer and meditation to the Hebrews after their return from Babylonian exile. They found the Holy City in ruins, poverty-stricken, and surrounded by hostile tribes. Haggai pointed out the futility of trying to produce outer results without first making inner contact with God: "Consider your ways. Ye have sown much, and bring in little; ye eat, but ye have not enough; ye drink, but ye are not filled with drink; ye clothe you, but there is none warm; and he that earneth wages earneth wages *to put it* into a bag with holes." Then Jehovah told them: "Consider your ways. Go up to the mountain, and bring wood, and build the house; and I will take pleasure in it."

In metaphysical language, the word *mountain* means a high place in thought, feeling, and prayer. When one gets back to that high place of peace and power in silent prayer and meditation, one accumulates "wood"—the substance of new thought, new energy, new power, new ideas—and is then able to "build the house," or produce the outer, visible results of good.

Moses, Elijah, and Jesus, among others, proved the practical, result-getting power of silent meditation. It was at the conclusion of Moses' forty-day period of prayer in the wilderness that he went forth and supervised the construction of the tabernacle, the Hebrews' first building of formal worship. Moses even received specific instructions about the rich, beautiful furnishings for this tabernacle from Jehovah, during his forty-day meditation period. At the conclusion of Elijah's forty days of prayer, he knew that Elisha was to become the next prophet of Israel; he also anointed a new king over Syria and one over Israel, to clear up the political confusion of that era. And it was after Jesus had prayed silently and meditated for forty days that He began to preach, heal, and teach.

H. Emilie Cady has described the power of meditation: "Every man must take time daily for quiet meditation. In daily meditation lies the secret of power.... You may be so busy with the doing, the outgoing of love to help others (which is unselfish and Godlike as far as it goes), that you find no time to go apart. But the command, or rather the invitation, is 'Come ye yourselves apart and rest a while.' And it is the only way in which you will ever gain definite knowledge, true wisdom, newness of experience, steadiness of purpose, or power to meet the unknown, which must come in all daily life."

She also tells how to meditate: "When you withdraw from the world for meditation, let it not be to think of yourself or your failures, but invariably to get all your thoughts centered on God and on your relation to the Creator and Upholder of the universe. Let all the little annoying cares and anxieties go for a while, and by effort, if need be, turn your thoughts away from them to some of the simple words of the Nazarene, or of the Psalmist. Think of some Truth statement, be it ever so simple. No person, unless he has practiced it, can know how it quiets all physical nervousness, all fear, all oversensitiveness, all the little raspings of everyday life—just this hour of calm, quiet waiting alone with God. Never let it be an hour of bondage, but always one of restfulness."

The Psalmist described meditation and silence as the "secret place of the Most High." Jesus spoke of it as going into the closet and shutting the door. Carlyle wrote: "Consider the significance of silence; it is boundless, never by meditating to be exhausted, unspeakably profitable to thee! Cease that chaotic hubbub, wherein thy soul runs to waste, to confused suicidal dislocation and stupor; out of silence comes thy strength."

After meditating upon God's goodness and being renewed, uplifted, and inspired with new ideas, there is an effective way to utilise meditation and silence in relation to your problems: Take any problem or question and meditate on this thought: *"There is a divine solution to this situation. I accept and claim the divine solution in this situation now."* The mental energy spent in worry and battling with the problem will then be used constructively to give you the right ideas and right solution. When you have a problem, if you will go into silent meditation and contemplate its solution from a divine standpoint, you will be shown what to do.

An engineering executive has told me of his use of meditation as a problem-solver. When his employees run into difficulty on an engineering project, he goes into his office, silently meditates on the problem from a divine standpoint, and inevitably gets the right ideas for its solution. One of his junior executives once asked him how he managed always to have the right answer just when it was needed most. When he explained his simple method, the junior executive skeptically asked, "You mean you just meditate on the solution, rather than fight the problem?" The engineering executive believes that the world is full of harried, tense people who have become that way through trying to solve problems in outer ways.

Let the practice of prayer, in one of the four forms, help you solve life's problems in inner, true ways. Let communion with God and His goodness open the way for greater peace, health, and plenty in you and in your world. The writer of the Third Epistle of John might have been describing the prospering power of prayer when he declared, "Beloved, I pray that in all things thou mayest prosper and be in health, even as thy soul prospereth."

CHAPTER 3

Making the Right Contact for Prosperity

In this era when success is erroneously considered by some to be the result of knowing the "right people" or having the "right contacts," it is refreshing to read these words of Charles Fillmore: "What we need to realize above all else is that God has provided for the most minute needs of our daily life and that if we lack anything it is because we have not used our mind in making the right contact with the supermind.... The spiritual substance from which comes all visible wealth is never depleted. It is right with you all the time and responds to your faith in it and your demands upon it."

True prosperity, then, is the result of making contact with the spiritual substance within the

God-mind of man. Furthermore, that substance will respond to our faith in it and our demands upon it. The most powerful method of making this contact, and yet the simplest, is through affirmative prayer.

We can have any good thing for which we are willing to pay the price of daily, consistent affirmation. But knowing "about" the power of affirmative prayer isn't enough; we have to pray affirmatively, personally and constantly. Our words are loaded with power, and every word we speak goes out and returns as a multiplied result. Knowing this, I like to affirm often, *"My words are charged with prospering power."*

There are various types of affirmative prayers that we may speak in making the right contact with the God-mind within us. To affirm is simply "to make firm," and affirmative prayers do just that—they make firm our good and help us experience it. One type of affirmative prayer is that of blessing. By blessing the substance at hand, we increase its flow and its immediate multiplying power. If a purse seems empty, we should take it in our hands and bless it by affirming, *"I bless you and bless you for the riches of God that are now being demonstrated in and through you."* As we eat our meals, it is good to bless our food. When we dress, we should bless our clothes.

Here are some of the affirmative prayers that I use daily—for perfect clothes: *"I give thanks that I am appropriately and divinely clothed with the rich substance of God"*; for a perfect home: *"I give thanks that I am appropriately and divinely housed with the rich substance of God"*; for perfect transportation: *"I give thanks that I am appropriately and divinely transported, wherever I wish to go, with the rich substance of God."*

Many businesswomen particularly like this affirmation: *"I give thanks for ever-increasing health, youth, and beauty, in the name of Jesus Christ."* Other affirmations of thanks that have proved powerful for many people are these—for increased income: *"I give thanks that my financial income increases mightily now, through the direct action of God"*; for payment of indebtedness and financial obligations: *"I give thanks for the immediate, complete payment of all financial obligations, in the name of Jesus Christ"*; for increased success along all lines: *"I give thanks that every day in every way I am growing richer and richer!"*

Recently a group of Unity students who had been studying the book *Both Riches and Honor*, by Annie Rix Militz, were asked to affirm the following prayer for harmony in their homes and businesses: *"Let there be peace within my walls and prosperity within my palaces."* They reported happy, peaceful results.

This same group was asked to affirm for new business and new customers: *"I love the highest and best in all people and I now draw the highest and best people* [customers, clients] *to me."* This prayer seemed to "click" with the entire group and produced exciting experiences. A salesman discovered that by speaking this prayer, he attracted into his department only people who really intended to buy and who did buy. Consistent use of this prayer also helped him to make a number of sales that he previously thought he had lost.

Another member of this group, a saleswoman who is employed in a store with more than a hundred employees, prayed this prayer with such great success that she led the entire store in sales. She was honored by her employers for having sold $44,000 worth of merchandise within a given period. Only three other salespeople in that store (all men) sold more than $30,000 worth of merchandise during the same period. This woman's department was one of the lower-priced merchandise areas, which necessitated her making many more individual sales.

Another affirmative prayer that this group found helpful was: *"Everything and everybody prospers me now."* A government employee who spoke this prayer daily was soon informed of an inheritance that had been available but unclaimed for a number of years. Another Unity student who was praying this prayer was one of eleven heirs who inherited a gravel pit in another State. Because of the number of heirs, the amount of money she received from this inheritance had been small. After faithfully affirming, "Everything and everybody prospers me now," her income checks from the gravel business began arriving monthly in larger and larger amounts. During the winter months, when this business was supposed to "slump," she received the largest income of all. She now has an increasing monthly income from her inheritance.

The owner of a local modeling school is now forming a chain of charm and modeling schools all over the South as a result of her successful use of affirmative prayer. She discovered after using this same prayer that she felt led to teach fewer classes than in the past. However, class attendance was larger and her classes were comprised of prosperous-minded students who paid for their courses on time or even ahead of time. Consequently her income steadily increased.

One member of this Unity group had long hoped to make a trip to Hawaii, to visit relatives stationed there with the armed forces. After affirming, "Everything and everybody prospers me now," not only did the way open for her to make the trip but her husband, a businessman, was also able to arrange a month away from his job. Together they flew to Hawaii and had a glorious month with their family.

After using this same affirmative prayer, a secretary felt led to sell and reinvest some securities she had inherited several years previously but which had not brought adequate compensation. After reinvesting them, she received immediate financial return on her securities.

Still another form of affirmative prayer is sincere praise. We should praise what we have, and in our thoughts and words we should insist that it is constantly expanding into greater good. We should also praise God for His goodness that is always at work in our lives. George Muller, who has been described as "the man of faith to whom God gave millions," once said:

"Expect great things of God and great things you will have. There is no limit to what He is able to do. Praise Him for everything. I have praised Him many times when He sent me ten cents and I have praised Him when He has sent me sixty thousand dollars, I have trusted Him for one dollar and I have trusted Him for thousands, and never in vain."

A wonderful way to express praise is to begin the day by affirming prosperity and success, instead of facing it with dread, fear, or tense anxiety. Praise has a happy, relaxing effect upon us and our world. In the early morning hours, send praise ahead of you into the day and insure its success by affirming: "*With praise and thanksgiving, I set the riches of God before me this day to guide, govern, protect, and prosper me. All things needful are now provided. My rich good becomes visible this day!*"

A stockbroker recently brought to my attention another type of affirmative prayer that helps him make the right contact for prosperity: affirmations of confidence. He stated that he has studied the prosperity law from every angle, observed the many prosperous-minded people who buy and sell stock, and read many biographies of the lives of prosperous-minded people. He has come to the conclusion that if prosperity could be described in one word, that word would be *self-confidence;* that is, confidence in one's abilities and talents, and in God's help in developing them.

Affirmative prayers that express confidence help us release our prosperity powers. Psychologists tell us that there is tremendous power in having self-confidence. They say that confidence doubles our powers and multiplies our abilities. We may more fully develop the prosperity power of confidence by affirming often, "*I am confident that God is my instant, constant, abundant supply of health, wealth and happiness,*" or, "*I am the richly illumined child of God, filled with divine love and wisdom, by which I am guided in all my ways and now led into that which is for my highest good.*"

A railroad employee was asked to repair a locomotive that no one else had been able to adjust. When he heard of the various mechanics who had attempted to repair this engine without success, he was almost overwhelmed. But then he remembered the power of affirmative prayer. Before beginning work, he went aside to a quiet place and from his wallet he took this affirmation and spoke it silently: "*I am a child of the living God, I am one with His wisdom; that wisdom now leads me in paths of righteousness, peace, and true success.*" As he was thinking of these words and letting them fill him with confidence, another employee passed through the shop and asked what he was doing, to which he replied that he was "going over a plan" that he intended to use in repairing the locomotive. Shortly thereafter, he returned to his work and quickly repaired the troublesome engine. Later the other employee asked him for a copy of the "plan" he had used with such quick success.

A certain executive was within a year of retirement, yet he did not feel that he was ready for a rocking chair. So he began praying that other divinely satisfying work would open to him. Since he did not know just what outer contacts to make to help bring forth such a result, he made none. Instead, he made the inner contact by spending a lot of time quietly affirming this prayer of confidence: "*The Spirit of the Lord goes before me, making easy and successful my way.*"

One day he received a telephone call from someone he had never met, offering him work in Florida, of the same type he had been handling. Within a week, he received a similar offer by mail. Prayers of confidence multiply not only our powers and our abilities, but also our opportunities. Within a short time, this man resigned his job, sold his home, and made the change into a new position that holds a limitless future for him—because he dared to affirm confidently, "*The Spirit of the Lord goes before me, making easy and successful my way.*"

If you have a prosperity need, be assured that you can make the "right contact" for prosperity. God has provided for the most minute needs of your daily life. If you lack anything, use your mind to make the right contact with the supermind of God within you. A postal employee who had to take an efficiency test affirmed, "*Divine Mind knows and Divine Mind shows.*" His test proved him most efficient.

Affirmative prayers that express praise, thanks, blessing, confidence, and rich ideas of good are powerful yet simple channels for making the right contact with the supermind of God within you for prosperity.

CHAPTER 4

Substance— the Key to Prosperity

What is substance? The dictionary describes it as "that which underlies all outward manifestations; real, unchanging essence or nature of a thing." Jesus might have been referring to omnipresent substance when He spoke of the kingdom of heaven being at hand. Metaphysicians have described substance as "mind essence" or "thought stuff."

Charles Fillmore said: "This inexhaustible mind substance is available at all times and in all places to those who have learned to lay hold of it in consciousness... The spiritual substance from which comes all visible wealth is never depleted. It is right with you all the time and responds to your faith in it and your demands upon it."

We are always molding inexhaustible mind substance through our mental concepts, whether we are aware of it or not. But often we mold tangible things, conditions, and experiences that we do not want, by holding concepts of disease, inharmony, old age, and financial lack.

We can consciously and deliberately take control of our world by taking control of our attitudes about substance. The truth about substance is that it is mind essence which is present in all, through all, and around all. But this indestructible, inexhaustible substance is handled by the thoughts of the mind, which make it useful as visible results.

We should constantly think of and appreciate substance, because substance contains every element of good: life, love, wisdom, power, all good. But since substance is passive, it waits upon man to form it as he will; it comes forth in man's world according to his thoughts and words of good or of limitation. The world was created in the beginning out of substance when Jehovah God said, "Let there be." We create our world out of substance in like manner.

If there seems to be dissatisfaction in any phase of your life, affirm: *"Divine substance is the one and only reality in my life, and I am now satisfied with divine substance."* For more definite needs declare: *"Divine substance appropriately manifests for me here and now."*

Still other powerful affirmations to help you mold substance as prosperous results are these: *"Divine substance cannot be diminished. Divine substance cannot be exhausted. Divine substance cannot be withheld. Divine substance cannot be taken. Divine substance is everywhere present, and I wisely use it now. Divine substance is the one and only reality and divine substance never fails to manifest. The finished results of divine substance now appear in rich, appropriate form."*

A businessman whose stock market transactions had been unsuccessful during the previous year found that, as he began to declare substance as the only reality in his financial affairs, his success began to manifest. Within two months, his profits were greater than in the previous twelve months.

The owner of a cleaning plant watched his business increase weekly after he began affirming substance as the only reality in his financial affairs (even though three other cleaning plants in the same area closed down during this period). In fact, this man's volume increased $400 a week over that of the preceding month, after he began thinking of substance as the key to his prosperity.

A housewife who received an annual income from a relative's estate did not receive her check at the usual time. After affirming divine substance as the one and only reality in her financial affairs, the check finally arrived—late, but three times as large as the previous year's check.

Another housewife was affirming divine substance as the one and only reality in the financial affairs of her husband, when he was offered the best engineering job he had ever had. Furthermore, his new employer insisted that his starting salary be $100 more per month than he was asking!

"Physical science has discovered that everything can be reduced to a few primal elements, and that if the universe were destroyed it could be built up again from a single cell." In like manner we can expand or rebuild our financial world from a single right attitude about substance.

A doctor proved the expanding power of right attitudes about substance. As he began to affirm that divine substance was the one and only reality in his financial affairs, an insurance company employed him to treat its company salesmen, his fees to be paid promptly by the company itself. This assignment was in addition to his already successful private practice.

As he continued to affirm substance as the one and only reality in his financial affairs, another interesting prosperity result appeared: Two years previously he had attempted to purchase a piece of business property, but the owner asked twice the amount the doctor felt led to pay. So the doctor dismissed the matter from his mind, thinking that if the property was his by divine right, he would be able to purchase it at the price he felt was right.

After he began affirming substance as the only reality, the owner of the property came to him and stated that he now wished to sell the business property. Having no other buyers, he was ready to sell it at the original price, which was half the amount he had been asking for the last two years—and exactly what the doctor had felt led to pay!

Charles Fillmore has given some good advice on how to realize substance as the key to your prosperity: "Daily concentration of mind on Spirit and its attributes will reveal that the elemental forces that make all material things are here in the ether awaiting our recognition and appropriation. It is not necessary to know all the details of the scientific law in order to demonstrate prosperity. Go into the silence daily at a stated time and concentrate on the substance of Spirit prepared for you from the foundation of the world. This opens up a current of thought that will bring prosperity into your affairs."

I have just read a news report about a young man who, though not yet thirty, has become vice-president of an insurance company. For several years he has made it a habit to concentrate daily on substance. This man realized several years ago the power of his thoughts and words for success or failure, and he began spending an hour every morning thinking about substance and molding it in definite detail with his thoughts. During this morning hour, he mentally planned his day as he wished it to be, and he held in mind the figures of sales he wished to obtain.

Later, when he was placed in charge of a group of insurance salesmen, he spent time each morning thinking of them and the amount of sales he wished them to make that day. It was by this daily, faithful process of molding substance as he wished it to be, for himself and for others, that he worked his way up to the vice-presidency of his company. It has been predicted that he will be a millionaire by the time he is thirty-five.

A housewife has described how daily meditation upon substance filled her grocery shelf. Prior to spending this time daily, she never had enough groceries on hand to feed the relatives and friends who often visited in her home. Then, as she began to meditate daily upon substance as the one and only reality, everyone who came to visit began bringing gifts of groceries and food. One relative began bringing fresh seafood from the coast where he lives. Another brought fresh bread, cakes, and pies from the bakery where he works. This woman says that now her freezer and pantry shelves are constantly filled with groceries.

With every silent thought, as well as with every spoken word, you are telling substance what to do, and it obediently carries out whatever beliefs you hold in mind about it. In your silent thoughts as well as in your spoken words, give your attention to the richness of substance. It will seem as though heaven and earth are working together to produce satisfying results for you.

One Unity student says that her money goes much further when she shops, if she is "dressed up." By wearing her best clothes, even when she shops at the corner grocery store, she has a feeling of being prosperous. Others who come in contact with her unconsciously think of her as prosperous, and give her the benefit of their attitudes. The result is that her money seems to go further, and she seems able to buy more. It is as though substance is pleased, and multiplies for her.

When you give substance your appreciative attention, it seems to work overtime in many ways to meet your needs. A salesman who heard a lecture on substance went out the next day and immediately made a $1,200 sale to a customer who had previously given him only very small orders.

By declaring substance to be the one and only reality, you can cause old, dissatisfying conditions to fade away. By declaring the satisfying reality of substance, you can cause your mind to be filled and strengthened with new ideas, and your body to be renewed with vitality, energy, and renewed health. By declaring substance as the only reality, you place yourself in a position to witness the riches of the universe as they flow to you on every hand, in whatever form is most appropriate at the moment.

A merchant once had a customer whose friendship he apparently had lost. The former business friend had been writing him unfriendly letters. Instead of retaliating, the merchant sat down and mentally reworked the situation as he wished it to be, seeing the customer as friendly and co-operative, rather than as he appeared at the moment.

The merchant also affirmed that divine substance was the one and only reality in the situation, and that divine substance would not fail to make the situation right for all concerned. When he was able after several quiet periods to get a genuine feeling of friendliness, kindness, and good will toward the other man, he wrote him a letter just the opposite of those received: words of kindness, stating the merchant's desire that their friendship and business association might continue. He wrote, "My wish for you and your business is happiness, prosperity, and abundant good, and my continued thought for you shall be for your prosperity."

It was not long before the other man's attitude had changed completely, and the two men found themselves in complete harmony again.

In fact, the merchant sold his friend $5,000 worth of merchandise shortly after this!

Conscious union between substance and man is made within the mind of man. Knowing this, you no longer need feel that something or somebody can keep your financial supply from you. Indeed, you begin to realize that through your right understanding of substance, all things can be accomplished within the mind first.

In my own experience, I have proved to my complete satisfaction the power that is generated by giving substance my conscious thought. In one instance, while I sat in my study completing some writing assignments that were due, I suddenly realized how hungry I was; but there seemed to be no time to go out and eat. So I affirmed: *"Divine substance is the one and only reality and divine substance never fails. The finished results of divine substance now appear in this situation in appropriate form."*

Within a few minutes I received a telephone call from a neighbor, whom I had never met. She had seen the light on in my study and realized I was working late. She wondered if I would consider sharing a meal she had already cooked; she said that if I would, she would send it over to me on a tray, while it was still warm. Within a few minutes from the time I had made my affirmation, I was enjoying a complete meal in my study, provided and prepared by someone I had never even met.

In another instance, I was thinking of new clothes. I had in mind a particular type of dress with matching jacket that was currently in fashion, but I had not the money with which to purchase it just then. Within a few days, after affirming substance as the one and only reality, a friend brought me, as a gift, the type of dress and jacket I wished, though it was far more beautiful than anything I had been able to visualize. In still another instance, when my son was in need of certain items of clothing, a friend telephoned late one night to say that she had a box of boy's clothes she wanted to give to him. She especially mentioned the items of clothing he needed as those that she had on hand in abundance, and said she would include these.

When we realize that we can gain control of substance through our attitudes, it is as though we gain control of our financial affairs, rather than feeling subject to them. As we gain this feeling of dominion, we no longer feel financially bound, limited, or discouraged; we know that we have the power to change whatever needs to be changed by changing our attitude about it. As we begin to appreciate rather than depreciate substance, it seems to begin working very hard to please us and to meet our needs. As we think of it as the one and only reality in our lives, substance then has the power to work for us in unlimited ways for our greatest good.

Charles Fillmore might have been summarizing the power of attitudes to mold substance when he wrote, "Substance is first given form in the mind."

Never underestimate the power of substance. It underlies everything in your world and it is controlled by your ideas about it. Whether it is life, love, wisdom, power, or more financial good that you want, give substance your wholehearted attention and appreciation. It will become your obedient servant, only too happy to work with you, for you, round about you—to provide for you in every way.

Substance is the one reality, and your understanding of this gives you the key to prosperity.

CHAPTER 5

The Prosperity Law of Increase

Outer use of the law of increase is simple and pleasant. It requires first the establishment and maintenance of an attitude of rich increase toward everybody and everything. Let your first thoughts, when thinking of others or contacting them by mail, by telephone, or in person, be thoughts and blessings of increase. Just thinking of a rich increase of good in connection with others helps them become more prosperous. They may not be consciously aware of your prosperous thoughts and blessings, but they will subconsciously receive them and be richly blessed.

The law of increase is what all people are seeking to invoke in one way or another. The universal desire for increase is nothing more than man's innate divinity seeking expression as fuller good in his life. Every man instinctively feels it and instinctively responds to some extent. All people are seeking more or better food, clothes, homes, beauty, knowledge, leisure, pleasure, luxury—increase in something. And rightly so! A normal desire for increased good is not to be condemned or suppressed. It is divine.

We should also convey the impression of increase with everything we do, so that others will receive that rich impression. The thought of blessing is the thought of increase. The prayer of increase releases it. Give this silent thought of increase, at every opportunity, to your family, social acquaintances, business associates, spiritual friends, world leaders, and all people everywhere: *"I bless you and bless you with a rich increase of God's almighty good."*

When you bless people, inanimate objects, situations, and appearances with the thought of increased good, then that person, object, situation, or appearance unconsciously receives the good of your blessing. You are richer for having given it; it will come back to you as a richly multiplied blessing. And the recipient is richer for having had your attention and your prosperous thought. This practice is much more satisfying than the reverse, which too many people practice: thinking of things and people as failures.

Another way to employ the law of increase is by blessing ourselves with an equal thought of increase. We can do this just by *feeling* that we are getting rich and that we are making others rich. Our every act, tone, and look should express a quiet, rich assurance. Words to convince others of our prosperity are not necessary when we get the feeling of richness implanted in our subconscious. The feeling can be radiated from us and communicated to others. They will then want to be associated with us in business transactions and otherwise, so as to benefit from our consciousness of prosperity.

Just by working quietly to attain a feeling of richness, we can draw to us prosperous-minded persons we have never seen before, who will become our customers and business associates. People unconsciously go where there is a consciousness of increase. It is thus that business increases rapidly, and many rich blessings flow to us. If we give the thought of increase to others and entertain it quietly in the deep recesses of our own minds, others are attracted to us and automatically help to prosper us.

Another way to invoke the law of increase is in regard to our work. We should do all that we can do every day, and we should do all of our work in an efficient manner. But the actual amount of work we do is not as important as our attitude about our work.

Let us put the thought of success in everything we do.

If you do not feel that you are in your right place or in congenial work, practice using the law of increase anyway. As you bless others and yourself with the thought of increase, people, ideas, and opportunities will be attracted to you, and new channels of success and advancement will open to you.

All of these mental attitudes are very important to prosperity. There is also something that we need to do in an outer way to expand our faith in God as the source of our prosperity: we should make Him our financial partner. When we touch upon this particular facet of the law of increase, our prosperity is constantly and divinely assured.

The outer facet of the law of increase is the spiritual law of tithing. Any practice that has been handed down through the centuries, as tithing has been, must have great importance. Some persons may study other prosperity laws and be prospered for a time; but accomplishment is invariably easier when the divine law of tithing is invoked. Those who tithe associate themselves with divine riches; it is as though all the forces of heaven and earth rush forth to guard, guide, and prosper them. Through tithing they go from success to greater success, almost effortlessly because they are divinely helped in their achieving.

In my own personal experience, prosperity proved elusive until I began tithing—at a time when I was making only $100 a month, supporting myself and my son, and helping my sister through college. The decision to tithe was not an easy one to make, but it was the wisest and most rewarding I have ever made.

A merchant in the furniture business recently told me that he had tithed at various times without satisfactory results; and that it was only after he heard a lecture on the importance of tithing to the spiritual organization or person from which one receives spiritual help, that he realized why he had not previously prospered. He had been tithing to a certain church to please his family, although he was not receiving the inspiration he needed from that church. He began tithing to the spiritual organization that was inspiring him—and the prosperous results in his business have reflected the change.

Recently a jeweler said to me: "Before I began the practice of tithing, I could not make ends meet. Now I find that I have enough to spare and to share." Another man who heard this conversation said: "Since I decided to tithe I have never hesitated to get what I want and enjoy it. I used to wonder if I could afford certain things, and I often went without the very things I should have been enjoying as a child of God. Since beginning to tithe, I have purchased what I wanted in the way of homes, cars, and clothes, and always I've been enriched. The practice of tithing first made me feel rich, and then the outer riches came."

A postal employee reports: "A relative of mine has the same income as I do, but he's in constant financial need. Recently when I offered to help, he said, 'How can you possibly help me when your income is practically the same income as mine?' I told him, 'The difference is that I tithe.' I think that if people would teach their children to tithe, the children would never have financial difficulties in later years."

A powerful prayer for daily use is: *"Voluntary, faithful tithing of my whole income brings ever-increasing prosperity to me, and through me to others."*

CHAPTER 6

Tithe Your Way to Prosperity

Charles Fillmore has written, "Tithing is based upon a law that cannot fail, and it is the surest way ever found to demonstrate plenty, for it is God's own law and way of giving." The truth of this has been proved again and again. I once knew two professional men who were partners. One tithed; the other did not. The one who did not tithe made around twenty thousand dollars a year. He worked nights, days, and weekends, and still could not "get by" financially. There were frequent spells of illness and unexpected mishaps in his family. The harder he worked, the more he had to work. Collecting money owed him was difficult.

His business associate made about twelve thousand dollars a year, and he tithed. He seemed to live much better; his family seemed to have more. Surely they enjoyed life more. This man never thought of working nights or weekends; his clients liked him and paid their accounts without protest or delay. Finally, after several years, he left the partnership and went out on his own. Soon he was making a great deal more money than his former partner made. He put God first financially, and the Lord prospered him.

Charles Fillmore has further written: "By the act of tithing men make God their partner in their financial transactions and thus keep the channel open from the source in the ideal to the manifestation in the realm of things. Whoever thinks that he is helping to keep God's work going in the earth cannot help but believe that God will help him. This virtually makes God not only a silent partner but also active in producing capital from unseen and unknown sources, in opening up avenues for commercial gain, and in various other ways making the individual prosperous."

A woman recently told me that she and another member of her family held identical shares of stock. During a time of financial stress, she decided to sell her stock; she made only a few hundred dollars' profit from the sale. The other member of the family, who tithed faithfully from all channels of income, prayed for guidance and decided to hold his stock a little longer. A few weeks later he sold it for a profit of $6,000! This woman now realizes that if she, too, had had faith in the tithing law of prosperity, expecting it to prosper and protect her, guidance would have come, meeting her financial need in some other way, so that she also would have made a $6,000 profit, instead of only a few hundred dollars. Needless to say, she is now a consistent tither of all her income.

L. E. Meyer says in *As You Tithe So You Prosper* that we make things at least ten times easier when we honor the Lord with our tithe; that in tithing we substitute faith in God's supply for fear that we shall come to want; and that tithing is a law of financial liberty. He has written: "The story of tithing both ancient and modern declares it to be the best investment we can make. It does more good than the most generous giving that is done only on the impulse of the moment." And we can see why: Just as it is necessary to breathe out regularly in order to receive fresh air into the lungs, so it is necessary to give regularly if we wish to receive regularly. From a business standpoint, we prefer a definite, systematic, regular income to an occasional, undetermined inflow of money, which may or may not be financially sufficient. "Whatsoever a man soweth, that shall he also reap." If we do not sow, we do not reap.

In loosing the purse strings we loose many other things that have bound us, so that we are free from the unhappy, unnecessary, unwanted experiences of life. I know from my own experience how much healthier I have been since I began tithing a decade ago. As a result, I am now able to produce much more work in a much shorter time than I was previously able to do. Whenever I hear of loss, theft, accident, illness, and the high emotional and financial costs that usually accompany these experiences, I cannot help thinking: "It's too bad those persons do not tithe. They would doubtless be protected from such negative and unhappy experiences."

Truly the Bible gives us the promise of prosperity and protection when we tithe. The first instance of tithing is found in the life of Abram, who tithed a "tenth of all" to the priest, Melchizedek (and the tenth must have been a considerable amount, because Abram was described as "very rich in cattle, in silver, and in gold").

Abram apparently passed along his belief in the prosperity law of tithing, because his grandson Jacob knew of its power. After Jacob left his father's house and went forth to seek his fortune in a new land, he made a prosperity covenant with the Lord: "If God will be with me, and will keep me in this way that I go, and will give me bread to eat, and raiment to put on, so that I come again to my father's house in peace, and Jehovah will be my God, . . . of all that thou shalt give me I will surely give the tenth unto thee."

In this passage Jacob clearly indicated that he expected his practice of tithing to protect and prosper him, as well as to reestablish harmony between himself and his family. The Bible reveals that all these blessings and more came to Jacob: "And the man increased exceedingly, and had large flocks, and maid-servants and men-servants, and camels and asses." When he later decided to return to the land of his birth and to attempt reconciliation with his brother Esau, whose birthright he had earlier stolen, he sent ahead rich gifts to Esau. When he and his brother were reconciled, Esau tried to return the gifts to Jacob; but Jacob said, "Take, I pray thee, my gift that is brought to thee; because God hath dealt graciously with me."

Throughout the Bible the tithe is mentioned as a "tenth of all," because ten was considered by the ancients to be a mystical number symbolizing increase. Solomon, whose great wealth is familiar to us, emphasized the prospering power of giving first of one's income, rather than waiting until other needs have been met, when he said:

"Honor Jehovah with thy substance, and with the first-fruits of all thine increase: so shall thy barns be filled with plenty, and thy vats shall overflow with new wine."

As long as the Hebrews tithed and honored the Lord with a tenth of all their income, they were prospered. However, it was pointed out during the Restoration Period by the prophet Malachi that because they were no longer tithing they had fallen into hard times. During this period, corruption was prevalent in every form: the Hebrews were intermarrying with other groups who did not worship Jehovah; there was a high divorce rate; deceit, robbery, and all types of violence were prevalent. Malachi pointed out that better times would again come if the people would again put God first financially: "Bring ye the whole tithe into the storehouse, . . . and prove me now herewith, saith Jehovah of hosts, if I will not open you the windows of heaven, and pour you out a blessing, that there shall not be room enough to receive it." Malachi promised not only renewed blessings of prosperity but renewed protection for their crops: "And I will rebuke the devourer for your sakes, and he shall not destroy the fruits of your ground; neither shall your vine cast its fruit before the time in the field. . . . And all nations shall call you happy; for ye shall be a delightsome land, saith Jehovah of hosts."

Sometimes people say, "Well, I'm not under the Old Testament laws, because I'm a Christian, and I follow only the Jesus Christ teachings." Of course as Christians we believe in and apply the spiritual teachings of the entire Bible. However, Jesus Christ also set forth the prosperity law of tithing. During New Testament times the temple (as well as the later work of the early Christians) was supported by tithes. Jesus clearly indicated His belief in tithing in parable; and once, when addressing a group of Pharisees, He made it plain that His followers should establish the right attitude toward tithing: "Ye tithe mint and anise and cumin, and have left undone the weightier matters of the law, justice, and mercy, and faith: but these ye ought to have done, and not to have left the other undone."

Paul pointed out that if the early Christians gave consistently, it would not be necessary to take offerings for his journeys: "Upon the first day of the week let each one of you lay by him in store, as he may prosper, that no collections be made when I come." And in a letter to the Hebrews, he makes mention of Abram's act of tithing.

The prosperity of any individual, nation, or organization that tithes rests on a firm foundation. Jesus might have been summarizing the power of the prosperity law of tithing when He advised: "Give, and it shall be given unto you; good measure, pressed down, shaken together, running over, shall they give into your bosom. For with what measure ye mete it shall be measured to you again."

Whatever your financial condition of the moment—even if, like the Children of Israel, you are in a financial wilderness or a state of financial dissatisfaction—you can be prosperous. You need not wait until "things get better" or until you "get out of debt" to begin living under the prosperity law of tithing. Right now, you should begin bringing divine order into your affairs by honoring God with a "tenth of all" income, as soon as you receive it. You can be assured that, like the Children of Israel, you will be led into the Promised Land of greater prosperity.

If you are already prosperous and successful, you can be assured that you shall remain so as long as you put God first financially. If the time ever comes when you feel that your tithe is "too much" or that you can no longer afford to give so much, simply put such thoughts out of your mind. If you stop tithing, you may find yourself back in a financial wilderness, with your income greatly diminished. This can be avoided by continuing to give a "tenth of all," regardless of the amount. Indeed, if your tithe becomes large, praise and give thanks that you have so much to give. "He who practices tithing will have more to give than he thought possible before."

One of the greatest fears of many wealthy people is the fear of losing their money. I once knew a millionaire in the construction business who literally worried himself into ill health, according to his doctors, though to all appearances he had nothing to worry about. It took me only a few minutes in conversing with him to discover that his greatest concern was about losing his money. Since the prosperity law of tithing promises protection in every way, no such fear assails those who tithe.

No matter where you are on the ladder of success, why not follow the example of Jacob, who made a definite prosperity covenant with the Lord? You might even paraphrase his words in writing out your own covenant or agreement with the Lord: "Knowing that God will be with me, and will help me attain the success and prosperity that I know are mine by divine right—the perfect supply of food, clothing, housing, and property that are divinely mine—so that my life may be fruitful and satisfying, and so that harmony, peace, good health, and prosperity shall reign supreme . . . for all these blessings and for all other blessings with which I am and shall be divinely endowed, I will begin immediately to give a tenth of all my income to God's work. I will gladly honor the Lord with my substance and with the first fruits of all my increase."

If you wish to simplify your prosperity agreement, you may write out and affirm often the last statement of Jacob's covenant: "Of all that thou shalt give me, I will surely give the tenth unto thee." Or you can use the words of Solomon: "I will honor the Lord with my substance and with the first fruits of all my increase."

Try making your covenant for a definite period—a month, six months, or a year. As a part of the agreement, you may want to list any definite results you wish to attain during that period, showing a definite future date by which you wish those results to unfold. Then place your written covenant in a safe place where no one will see or disturb it. Begin tithing immediately and regularly of the first fruits of all your increase, even before paying bills or meeting needs of any kind. At regular intervals, perhaps once a month, check your written covenant to see what listed results have been obtained, marking them off your list and giving thanks. At the conclusion of your first covenant period, you will be ready to venture forth and make another covenant with the Lord, concerning your prosperity plans, hopes, and desires for another stipulated period, and continue tithing, giving thanks to God for each result.

As you begin using this prosperity method of tithing and making a covenant with God concerning your financial affairs, you will probably become so fascinated with its power for progress and achievement that you will want to increase your tithe another ten percent. Joel Goldsmith has written: "Interestingly enough, rarely does tithing stop at ten percent. I have known three different people who tithed eighty percent of all their income and, surprising as it may seem, these people had more left to live on, and with, than they could possibly spend even if they were very extravagant."

CHAPTER 7

There Is Magic in It

I must admit that the first time I read these words written by Charles Fillmore in his book *Prosperity,* I was skeptical about their practical value: "Tell me what kind of thoughts you are holding about yourself and your neighbors and I can tell you just what you may expect in the way of health, finances, and harmony.... You cannot love and trust in God if you hate and distrust men. The two ideas, love and hate, or trust and mistrust, simply cannot both be present in your mind at one time, and when you are entertaining one, you may be sure the other is absent. Trust other people and use the power that you accumulate from that act to trust God. There is magic in it: it works wonders; love and trust are dynamic, vital powers." These words are to be found in the chapter on indebtedness. I could not imagine love having anything to do with debt!

But love *does* have something to do with the dissolution of indebtedness. Recently, the owner of a furniture company in Alabama related one of his many experiences along this line:

This man had a customer who refused to pay for a washing machine purchased from his store. The finance company finally reclaimed it; then the customer came rushing into the furniture store and started screaming at the proprietor in vile language. This raging man weighed about two hundred and forty pounds, and he stood about six feet, three inches tall, whereas the store owner is a much smaller man. As the customer made his abusive accusations, the furniture dealer listened quietly; and whenever possible, he declared between accusations, "But [naming the man], I love you!" He made this statement dozens of times until finally the enraged customer left in utter disgust.

In about thirty minutes, however, he returned to apologize for his behavior, and to thank the furniture-store owner for the way he had dealt with the situation. The customer then explained that he had lost his last job because of his temper, which had caused him to assault a man who later had to be hospitalized.

He further stated that the way the dealer had handled the situation had turned the tide of his temper and made him see how foolish he had been. He promised that as soon as he found another job he would pay for the washing machine—and he did. He became a fine, stable customer of this dealer who says now that it was not easy to say to another man, especially a raging one, "I love you," but that he had found it well worth the effort.

A lawyer, who had also studied Charles Fillmore's book *Prosperity*, recently related that he collected two big accounts by releasing love and trust as dynamic, vital powers.

At the end of 1958, in going over his books, he found two especially large accounts still due. He recalled that Mr. Fillmore had written, "A thought of debt will produce debt." He reasoned that as long as he believed in debt, resented debt, or attached the thought of debt to himself or others, he would remain in debt and perhaps cause others to remain in debt. So, to overcome such negative thoughts, and also to invoke the power of love and trust, the lawyer made a mental note of the clients who owed him large amounts. He began blessing their names daily, each one separately, and sincerely erasing the idea of debt attached to each one.

After he had been using this system for a short time, the two clients who owed the large sums settled with him on the same day, one of them mailing his check for the full amount from a distant state.

Perhaps you, too, have been skeptical of the practical power of love, especially in regard to the dissolving of indebtedness. If so, I recommend that you study the chapter "God Will Pay Your Debts" in the book *Prosperity,* and apply its principles.

No longer do I doubt the wonder of love. Indeed, I have discovered that it is true that love and trust are dynamic, vital powers which seem to contain magic, and which work wonders!

CHAPTER 8

Wheel of Fortune

An engineer recently shared with me his own private success formula, which has brought forth great good for him. This man began his study of the spiritual laws of prosperity and how to apply them in a practical manner at a time when he had just been told of a job transfer. The transfer created a series of problems. He realized from his Truth study that it would be necessary for him to develop and apply confidence and faith in God, in the spiritual laws of prosperity, and in himself, in order to work out all the details of his change successfully.

So he began to compile his own success formula. His first step was to regard God as a rich, loving, all-providing Father. He wrote God a series of letters listing his various problems and stating his human inability to handle them alone. Every time a new problem arose concerning the job transfer, he wrote God another letter and, as the solution to each problem unfolded, he wrote God letters of thanks. In this way he developed faith in God's goodness, and his confidence in his own ability to work with God's prosperity laws increased.

At this point he heard a lecture at the local Unity Center on the use of Treasure Maps, and was fascinated with the idea as practical yet spiritual. However, he felt that something more businesslike would perhaps inspire the average businessperson to use this same powerful technique in a slightly different manner.

So he prayerfully designed a "wheel of fortune" which he also used in solving his own prosperity problems. On a large piece of cardboard, he drew a circle. In the very center he placed a picture of Jesus Christ. This formed the innermost part of his wheel of fortune.

Then he divided his circle into six parts: *Spiritual growth, health, work, possessions, finance,* and *vacation*. In each of the sectors he placed pictures of the results he desired to achieve in those activities.

For instance, in the *business* sector he pasted a picture concerning the perfect job he hoped to find as a result of his forthcoming transfer. In connection with his pictures he used this affirmation: "*I am stimulated by divine intelligence, impulsed by divine love, and guided by divine power into my right work, performing it in a perfect way for perfect pay. The divine plan of my life now takes shape in definite, concrete experiences, leading to perfect health, happiness, success, and prosperity.*"

In the *possessions* sector of his Wheel of Fortune, he pasted a picture of his present home, and with it, this affirmation: "*Divine intelligence directs the right buyer to this property. Everyone concerned is blessed by a just and orderly exchange of values.*" Then, in the same space, he placed the picture of a new home, with the words, "*Infinite Mind knows our need, knows where the right house is, and knows how to manifest it to us at the right time.*" To help his wife through the transition period of moving and readjustment, he placed her picture in this area too, in connection with this affirmation: "*My wife is now stimulated by divine intelligence, impulsed by divine love, and guided by divine power, manifesting in her every experience perfect health, happiness, abundance, and success."* For their ability to go forth to new experiences in faith, there was a picture of a door, and the affirmation, *"As one door closes, a bigger and better door opens."*

In the *vacation* sector he attached the picture of a sandy beach and ocean background, with this prayer: *"I give thanks for a divinely planned vacation, under divinely planned conditions, with divinely planned supply."* For his over-all prosperity he also added the affirmation, *"I am guided by infinite wisdom, and divine order is established in my finances."*

In the *spiritual growth* sector of the wheel, he affixed the picture of a church, in connection with which he wrote: *"I am grateful that faith abides in my heart, grounded in my belief that my life is one with the life divine. I am divinely guided to spiritual understanding and development."* Nearby, he also placed a picture of the Bible.

As this man's confidence in God and in himself developed, through daily letters to God, and through daily viewing his Wheel of Fortune and affirming the various prayers in connection with it, his problems gradually turned into happy solutions. He soon received an engineering appointment to a three-and-one-half-million-dollar construction job, with complete freedom of action, and responsibility only to the vice president of the company.

He became so confident that their present home would be sold on time that he and his wife visited the new job location in a distant state and immediately found the ideal place to live. They set a date to return to the old home and move their furniture, a date by which they confidently expected the former home to be sold, and even went so far in faith as to make plane reservations for that date.

Everything worked out just as they had stipulated. Their house was sold on time and their furniture moved to their new home on the date they had set.

Then, after getting settled, they took a vacation in a lovely tropical area where there were sandy beaches and miles of ocean. When they returned, they were guided to a Unity Center in their new location, as they had pictured it on their Wheel of Fortune.

This engineer truly proved the words of Goethe:

"What you can do, or dream you can, begin it; Boldness has genius, power and magic in it." He further proved to himself, in working with the spiritual laws of prosperity, a fact that he already knew to be true in his engineering profession from working with blueprints: Results have to be planned. Prosperity is a planned result, just as is every bridge that is built, every building that is constructed.

Your good can also come forth as a planned result if you will write daily notes to God concerning your success, and then prayerfully construct your Wheel of Fortune and use it daily. When we visualize with the help of a Treasure Map or a Wheel of Fortune, we are really praying and imaging our good; we are changing the current of our thinking from negative to positive, from despair to hope, from discouragement to encouragement.

CHAPTER 9

Harvest Your Good

The secret of harvesting our good is not to wait for joy or for good to come before we begin to praise God and to give thanks. If we wait for things to happen before we praise and give thanks, we may wait indefinitely. As spiritual beings, we should gain control of circumstances, events, and our own reactions to personalities. As spiritual beings we have the power to create our own circumstances, events, and environment. The secret is to sing, to rejoice, to praise, and to give thanks even before there seems to be anything for which to give thanks.

In the Unity pamphlet *Praise,* the author says that she was a chronic grumbler and that she stumbled on the hidden power of praise through the trial-and-error method. Her use of praise not only healed her body of pain, it healed her mind. She says: "I have proved to my satisfaction that praise will work along all lines. I have known praise to change even the face of nature, and to work what the ignorant call a miracle."

Most of us have seen the effect that praise has on animal and plant life. My mother always talked to and praised potted plants that were everywhere in her house. I always considered this one of mother's little habits, but now I know that her use of the spiritual principle of praise and blessing was her secret with her flowers. This secret caused her neighbors often to say that she had a green thumb.

We can harvest our good through praise, because words that express praise, thanks, and gratitude release energies within our mind and body. When we release energy through praise, we can be strong in body instead of weak. We can have peace and trust instead of fear, and we can have poise and power instead of shattered nerves. Myrtle Fillmore had talked to, had blessed, and had praised her body temple constantly for two years, and she finally brought forth health where there had been the indications of an incurable disease.

Praise and the giving of thanks enable us to liberate or to release the spiritual power that is within us. We are all filled with a dynamic force, whether we are aware of it or not. This dynamic force is spiritual power, and this power is constantly seeking release. What the modern world often calls tension is nothing but man's spiritual power that has not found proper release and expression. Tense, nervous, and high-strung persons would have increased spiritual power and could do greater and more wonderful things by consistently praising their minds, bodies, and affairs, for praise releases the inner spiritual power that lies within each of us.

Praise increases that to which it is directed. Praise draws and accumulates spiritual substance, and continual praise can bring forth prosperity. Praise draws and accumulates spiritual life, and continual praise can result in healing. Praise draws and accumulates knowledge, and it can bring forth guidance and help for any problem. Praise can open a new, wonderful world to us, because praise draws and accumulates good and gives it power for expression.

The whole creation responds to praise and is glad. We can praise our own ability, and our very brain cells will expand or increase in capacity when we speak to them words of encouragement and appreciation. When we feel discouraged, it is good to give ourselves a treatment in praise. This treatment changes our "I can't" attitudes and feelings so that they become "I can and I will" attitudes and feelings.

I recently heard someone compare an affirmation to a steering wheel in an auto. The steering wheel helps us to go in the right direction. Affirmations of praise also do this. They give us the desire to get started in the right direction and then they guide us on our way.

When we praise the riches or opulence of our loving Father, our mental atmosphere is greatly increased to receive these riches. Our wider mental outlook on riches opens the way for a richer supply. Through a persistent use of praise, a failing business can become a successful one, for even inanimate objects seem to respond to praise.

A woman once used the power of praise on her sewing machine, which was out of order. After she used words of praise, her sewing machine gave her no more trouble.

Another woman had a rag rug on her living room floor. For years she had been hoping for a new one. She heard of the law of praise and began to praise her old rug. Within two weeks a new one appeared from an unexpected source.

One of my associates recently related how the power of praise and blessing worked on a watch he was trying to repair. After he had done all that he could to repair the watch, my associate placed it on a shelf, blessed it, praised it, and left it for several days. When he inspected it later, he found that the watch ran perfectly.

The pamphlet *Praise* also suggests that we praise the qualities we would like to see in others, declare that others possess them already, and then see how quickly these persons will respond.

The author of this pamphlet says: "Since I have adopted the praise method, there has been a great change in all my household. I no longer censure my help for apparent carelessness and for accidents, but I excuse the accident in some pleasant way and praise help for their good intentions, their faithfulness, and their goodness. Thus I call into activity the very qualities that I recognize, and I make them strong and potent and abiding."

A person often thinks, "When I have this or when I am able to do that, then I will be happy."

But happiness does not come in these ways. Happiness already exists as a part of our divine nature. Through praise and thanksgiving we release this happiness.

All of us are surrounded by a pulsating energy which Jesus called the kingdom of the heavens. Out of this universal energy we can form and make whatever we want. We can use this universal substance all the time to form and to make our world. When our thoughts are not the highest, we have to live with results that are not the best. But each of us has the spiritual power to form this pulsating, radiant substance into good in his mind, body, and affairs.

All our words and attitudes affect us. Every time we sing, pray, or praise, we are carrying out the creative law. If we would be successful and happy, we must be very careful how we talk or listen to others talk about failure. This can keep us from experiencing success. In like manner, if we want to experience health, we must praise health and bless it until it becomes apparent in our body temple. We should talk health to our children and to our associates.

It is by man's word of praise and blessing that his world is restored to its perfection. The Children of Israel were shown that their sufferings and afflictions came not because God willed them but because they were disobedient to the law of praise. In Deuteronomy we read:

"All these curses shall come upon thee, and shall pursue thee, and overtake thee . . . Because thou servedst not Jehovah thy God with joyfulness, and with gladness of heart, by reason of the abundance of all things."

The Bible records many instances where Jesus gave thanks. Before He multiplied the loaves and the fishes, He gave thanks. At the grave of Lazarus, He said, "Father, I thank thee that thou heardest me." Note that He gave thanks before the answer appeared.

We can harvest our good through praise and thanksgiving. Our good awaits us, and through praise we make divine connection with it at just the right moment. Day by day we experience more and more of God's rich good through harvesting it with our thoughts, words, and declarations of praise.

The way to have an abundant harvest of good is to render praise and thanksgiving for the good we are entitled to as spiritual beings, even before there is any sign of it. Another way to increase our harvest of good is to praise and give thanks for the good we already have. Try it!

CHAPTER 10

Prosperity, the Hope of the World

Most of the world's ills (war, crime, vice, immorality, and disease) result directly or indirectly from prosperity's opposite: poverty. A doctor of my acquaintance states that he would have few patients were it not for financial problems that cause worry, strain, tension, and ill health.

Communism often gains a foothold because of poverty. A news story recently pointed out that Hungary fell to the communists a few years ago because at that time Hungary was the most poverty-stricken country in Europe. On the other hand, a recent editorial declared that because of the "growing prosperity" in eastern Europe, the threat of communism has lessened there. Another news item suggested that the president of the World Bank be nominated for the Nobel Peace Prize because of his efforts to promote financial adjustments in a number of countries. The article concluded, "Wouldn't it be timely to recognize that the proper use of cold cash can be a big factor for peace in the world."

Many religious leaders and writers long have been aware that poverty is among the world's besetting sins and the cause of many of the world's greatest problems. Charles Fillmore once wrote: "The Father's desire for us is unlimited good, not merely the means of a meager existence.... We cannot be very happy if we are poor, and nobody needs to be poor. It is a sin to be poor." And Georgiana Tree West has written, "Poverty is a form of hell, caused by blindness to God's good."

You and I are citizens of the world, and the whole world is influenced by our thinking. Let us set our thinking straight on the all-important subject of prosperity, so that we may help ourselves and all mankind. The truth about prosperity is this: Financial needs are really spiritual needs that must be met on a spiritual and a mental level, as well as on a physical level, before poverty can be permanently eradicated from the world. Charles Fillmore told how to meet prosperity needs when he wrote: "Some people think of prosperity as something separate from their spiritual experience, 'outside the pale' of religion. They live in two worlds: in one for six days of the week when man runs things, and in the other on the seventh day when God is given a chance to show what He can do. It is personality's demonstration when people find themselves complaining of hard times and depression, but it is not the way to demonstrate God in the fullness of all things. Do all things to the glory of God seven days a week rather than one. Take God into all your affairs. Use this thought: . . . *'I trust Thy universal law of prosperity in all my affairs.'*"

Our attitudes contain the key to our prosperity or lack of it. Richard Lynch describes what our attitudes should be in the face of apparent lack: "When business conditions have so receded as to seem hopeless; when the negative expressions of lack and loss and failure have prevailed, and since their action has been so far backward, reaction is bound to swing the pendulum in the opposite direction with equal force. For every negative state, its positive reaction. Plenty in the same degree that lack appeared; gain in place of loss; success and prosperity equal in force and quantity to the discouragement and failure of their antecedent action."

Man's attitudes can produce either prosperity or poverty for him; man *does* produce tangible things from the substance of his thought. A salesman told me that he had observed a friend, who is a very successful salesman, in a rural area of the Deep South. This fellow salesman does not have a large or particularly rich clientele, yet he always seems prosperous and happy. My friend discovered that the other salesman always has a standard answer when people ask him about business: "Business is wonderful because there's gold dust in the air!" And for him this seems to be true; every contact seems to result in a sale.

A saleswoman recently pointed out what the opposite attitude can do. She spoke of another woman who constantly talked lack and hard times, spending her lunch hours roaming about town, talking with other failure-minded people. When she returned to her job after lunch she always said the same thing: "I've been in stores all over town. Business is terrible. Nobody is selling a thing." Needless to say, this woman was not making her quota of sales. The result was that finally the manager of the store called her in and placed her on part-time work.

If we dare to declare, "There's gold dust in the air," we have the support of many economists who have predicted that this decade will be the "Golden Sixties." Periods of apparent recession are actually periods of readjustment; and, as Richard Lynch has pointed out, they cannot last, because the pendulum is bound to swing in the opposite direction with equal force. Balance is the law of the universe. As it works in the ebb and flow of the tides, in the varying seasons of the year, in day following night, so it must work in harmonizing the economic conditions of the world.

This should be a decade of rich blessings and great prosperity for all of us. If it is not as yet, perhaps we should check our attitudes. Earl Shaub has written, "We get what we want if we have faith, and we get what we don't want if we have fear.... There is no record of God ever saying to His heavenly host, 'We will have to get along on less for the duration of the slump. Things are dull through this gap and we had to lay off more angels last week. We will probably have to ration some of the necessities of life until we can work out of our trouble. We might even turn off a few stars to save light.'" Of course God never "talks hard times"; and as God's highest creations and heirs to His riches, there is no need for us to talk hard times or to experience them.

The prosperity of the years ahead awaits our recognition. It is the hope of our own well-being, and for the well-being of all mankind. We have a spiritual obligation to the world as well as to ourselves to think, talk, and affirm prosperity. Emma Curtis Hopkins pointed this out when she wrote, "There must be a free giving of your Truth, or the world may wait another million years for the wretched poverty of its people to be gone."

All prosperity comes from universal substance, which expresses through ideas. Thus, if we think and speak poverty ideas, substance produces poverty results; but if we think and speak prosperously, the substance of thought produces prosperous results for us. We are our results made manifest, and we have perfect freedom to experience lack or abundance. You might like to affirm: "*I trust the universal Spirit of prosperity in all my affairs. I am always provided for because I have faith in God as my omnipresent abundance.*"

This is a powerful prosperity prayer to use for others, too. A woman constantly talked prosperity and success to her husband during the depression years, at a time when his job was that of a day laborer. Though he was well educated, there seemed to be no openings in his field. While a number of persons regarded him as a failure, his wife always spoke in terms of the success that would come to him, of the interesting positions he would have, the good pay, the traveling, and of the prosperous life they would have together. It all seemed a faraway dream at the time, but this woman persisted in thinking and speaking prosperously to her husband, about him, and about their life.

Soon he obtained better work, and gradually he began to climb up the ladder of success. Every step of the way his wife continued to declare: "You can do it. You have what it takes." He began to think prosperously and confidently, too. After World War II, he became an executive for a leading corporation. Along with the most interesting work he had ever had, he was given a liberal expense account, an income that made it possible for his family to live in the lap of luxury, and the opportunity to travel all over the world and meet the world's famous and successful people. Even then his wife continued speaking prosperously to him, declaring for each job assignment: "You can do it. You have what it takes to do it."

Our attitudes and our words of prosperity and success can mean everything to others as well as to ourselves. For the people of the earth and for all nations, we might affirm words of prosperity and success by adapting the words of the 23d Psalm: "The Lord is your shepherd; you shall not want." Or we might paraphrase the affirmation suggested above: *"You trust in the universal Spirit of prosperity in all your affairs. You are always provided for, because you have faith in God as your omnipresent abundance."* Always, for ourselves and for all people, we should joyously affirm the words of Nehemiah, *"The God of heaven, he will prosper us."*

CHAPTER 11

What You Can Do about World Peace

Perhaps as you read your newspaper and listen to radio and television news reports, you are inclined to feel hopeless and helpless about world affairs. When such fears seem to well up within you, it is good to remind yourself that, as a recent magazine advertisement points out, "Our destiny is in our hands." This same advertisement also quoted from the charter of UNESCO: "Since wars begin in the minds of men, it is in the minds of men that the defenses of peace must be constructed." In other words, our thoughts, feelings, opinions, and prayers can be "secret weapons" for world peace.

Of course, pessimists will quickly disagree. They will tell you that we are doomed to destruction. But as you read the history of mankind, you will realize that the pessimists of all ages have predicted similar doom.

On the other hand, the faith-filled thinkers of this era will tell you that this is the most wonderful age the world has ever known. They maintain that this is an age of new enlightenment; an age of amazing scientific discovery, as well as an age of gratifying spiritual revival. Indeed, it has been claimed that more progress has been made on this planet in the last hundred years than in the preceding ten thousand years! Modern wonders are apparently only the first achievements of our accelerated progress.

In spite of the many challenges we now face, individually and collectively, in these times, truly this is an age of remarkable spiritual progress as well as scientific and economic achievement. In lecturing, in correspondence, as well as in private contact with countless others, I have discovered that the average person wears a mask and often does not speak much of the things nearest and dearest his heart. But I have been pleased to discover that when the masks are down, there are more really praying, faith-filled persons than this world imagines. Certainly such persons are the hope of peace and continued universal progress in this "space age."

I believe that the general public is now realizing and using the spiritual powers of faith and prayer to a greater extent than at any time in the last thousand years.

Recently, when speaking to a group of college students on various phases of practical Christianity in connection with daily, successful living, I discovered that their greatest desire was to know how to pray more effectively. When I offered to leave with them a number of printed affirmative prayers to meet various life problems, I was astonished at how quickly, after the lecture, they rushed forward and picked up every leaflet that I had available.

A prominent businesswoman has often driven several hundred miles for private discussion of her problems from a spiritual standpoint. I shall never forget how surprised I was in our first consultation when, in the midst of silent meditation concerning her problems, she started praying aloud for me!

Not long ago I visited a prayer group whose only purpose is to pray for world peace. This group consists of several housewives and two businessmen who get together one day a week at noon. They place a world globe in their midst, bless the troubled spots in the current news, and then pray for world peace. There are many private groups, such as this one, as well as countless organized church groups, who quietly gather regularly to pray for peace. A prominent West Coast minister recently stated that there are eight hundred people in his church prayer panel who pray daily at home at a stated time, and meet once a month to pray together, for world peace.

Recent mail has brought letters from a leper in a colony in the Philippines, from a young Negro in the troubled Congo, from a worker among the poor in India, from a schoolteacher in Belgium and from another in Italy, from a businesswoman in Bermuda, and from a professional man in Brazil. All of these letters spoke of the power of prayer, and of the writers' desire to invoke prayer more effectively in private matters, business affairs, and world conditions.

Some months ago a doctor wrote, after having received his call to active military duty: "I know the power of prayer works to produce good for people, situations, and events. Through the power of affirmative prayer as shown in *Good*

Business magazine, I have recently been greatly prospered, have become an effective physician able to render help to countless people. But now I am being recalled to active duty. This means I must leave my wife and family, as well as my practice. Somehow I know that prayer can help me make this adjustment, though at present I can see no good in this unexpected experience that has come into my life."

I suggested that he use this affirmative statement as he returned to active service for his country: *"New doors of good now open to me. With a confident spirit, I go forth into experiences of happiness, prosperity, and abundant living."* It was also suggested that he affirm that the divine plan for his life was unfolding in perfect ways, blessing all concerned. This he did, though perhaps with a heavy heart. Word has been received from him in recent weeks declaring that after he invoked affirmative attitudes through affirmative prayer, a very fine doctor appeared who is competently handling his practice while he is away; he has had some interesting and meaningful experiences in the service; and word has recently been received that he, along with a number of other reservists, will probably be released from active duty soon.

Affirmative prayer and affirmative attitudes constitute a "secret weapon" for individual peace as well as for world peace. A Chinese doctor, convinced of the power of prayer, has printed and mailed out 150,000 copies of his own worldwide prayer program, giving specific prayers to use for world peace. He furnished with this prayer program a synchronizing table, showing how people in all countries can pray at the same time for peace. He believes that only five minutes a day spent in prayer and meditation for peace can be more effective than feeding five hundred people or lecturing on religion for five hours.

A business executive recently stressed the importance of the individual and of the individual's affirmative attitudes, when he wrote: "We're paying a great deal of attention to our atomic and outer space race. I hope you and I don't think this is strictly the scientists' show and leave it all to them. The individual citizen and his personal efforts are still going to decide whether the world will be free or slave. We're the secret weapons in world peace and world power. Let us not forget it."

Your daily faith-quickened attitudes, words, and prayers for world harmony can have a greater influence for good on the world than you may now imagine. Indeed, faith-filled, affirmative prayer and positive attitudes may be the strongest links we have with atomic power in modern times. Charles Fillmore once wrote, "There must be a change of mind by the people of the earth before the tremendous uplift to be wrought by atomic energy can become beneficial and permanent.... We should therefore redouble our efforts to show man that the power that rules the world is within him."

The individual's power of thought has long been recognized. Forty years before the birth of Jesus, Manilius, a famous Roman, wrote: "No barriers, no masses of matter, however enormous, can withstand the powers of the mind. The remotest corners yield to them; all things succumb, the very heaven itself is laid open."

What are some of the atomic, faith-filled attitudes of mind we can establish and maintain as secret weapons for world peace? By what attitudes may we reach the remotest corners of the earth in behalf of world harmony?

First: Know that peace begins at home, within the "inner space" of your attitudes and private world. It does little good to hope, pray, or work for world peace when you live in constant conflict within yourself. A popular song that is being sung by church, college, and club groups everywhere contains this line: "Let there be peace on earth, and let it begin with me." In your own life—family group, business affairs, neighborhood and community—is the place to begin.

For instance, try giving praise instead of criticism to your family, business associates, and friends. This will do wonders to produce peace close at hand. We hear a lot about the starving people in various parts of the world, but there are plenty of persons nearby who are starving for sincere praise and appreciation. A housewife recently testified that praise had literally eliminated pain from her body, as well as trouble from her mind. It also transformed the atmosphere of her home, which had previously been steeped in chronic grumbling, fault finding, and complaining. Especially did praise produce a harmonious relationship with her husband and children.

A school teacher happily observed that her husband made a quick comeback in his business, which had been on the verge of bankruptcy, after she began speaking words of praise and appreciation to him. His health quickly improved, too, and all his previous talk of suicide stopped. He was like a new person.

David must have realized that peace begins at home when he decreed, "Peace be within thy walls, and prosperity within thy palaces."

A businessman once adopted this as a prayer, affirming for his office workers, *"Let there be peace within thy walls and prosperity within thy palaces."* Office bickering, jealousies, and inharmony subsided in a most satisfying way.

Second: In like manner, instead of criticizing and condemning community, civic, church, school, or political activities, make yourself part of them in positive action for betterment, if possible. If your circumstances do not allow active participation, at least give others the benefit of your praise for the good they are attempting to do. You might wish to paraphrase the words of the song for peace, declaring, *"Let there be peace on earth, and let it begin here and now."*

Also, instead of fretting about the wisdom of various moves our leaders make in negotiations for peace, remind yourself that our country's experts are constantly studying world affairs from every standpoint and that our national leaders follow the highest and best guidance they can obtain. Since the general public can never know all the behind-the-scene and often secret factors that enter into each decision, the public has no right to judge critically our leaders' decisions. In the words of Solomon, decree that our leaders be given "an understanding heart" to "discern between good and evil." If you have definite suggestions or information that may prove helpful in such matters, feel free to write to your officials.

Third: Learn to look at the people of the world (no matter how uncooperative some of them may appear in their hostile and warlike behavior) not as hopeless and eternally sinful, but as incomplete in their spiritual understanding and development. It is somehow easier, when you establish this viewpoint, to know that underneath a hard, aggressive, cruel exterior, they are also seeking their good, just as you and I are. With Job, seek to realize for them, ". . . there is a spirit in man, And the breath of the Almighty giveth them understanding."

Our government should not become lax in its persistent work and firm attitudes toward world peace. Your own high vision for mankind can help support all that is now being done on the political and diplomatic scenes to establish and maintain world peace.

Fourth: When the President, Secretary of State, Ambassador to the United Nations, or other of our country's leaders meet and talk with other world leaders, give all involved your very special blessing: "*I bless you and bless you for the goodness of God that is now mightily working in and through you to establish peace for all mankind,*" Dare to think of the leaders of the free world as being accompanied by a guardian angel, guiding, protecting, and instructing them. Bless these leaders with the words of the Psalmist:

"*. . . he will give his angels charge over thee, To keep thee in all thy ways. . . . Lest thou dash thy foot against a stone.*"

To all who ask how to pray for world peace, Silent Unity suggests these prayers:

For world peace. "*Let liberty, justice, peace, love, and understanding be established throughout the world, in the name of the Lord Jesus Christ.*"

For world leaders: "*Through the Christ Mind you are united in purpose, quickened to new understanding, and inspired to right action for the security and progress of all nations.*"

For the people of the world: "*There is but one presence and one power in the universe, God, the good Omnipotent. All the forces of good are working in men and nations. Peace, love, and understanding are uniting all people in one good world."*

For protection: *"The light of God surrounds you; the love of God infolds you; the power of God protects you; the presence of God watches over you; wherever you are, God is!"*

Fifth: Do not let anyone tell you that this is a hopeless time. This is an evolutionary time—a time of exploring many "new frontiers." This is an era of accelerated progress and achievement along all lines. Government, industry, management and labor, religions, science, education, and mankind in general are evolving toward greater understanding. Because of this you cannot judge them by their present development, which is ever changing and in the final analysis is improving (though it may not appear so to you at the moment).

Establish and maintain the attitude that in spite of all the challenges of this era, the "space age" is a great time to be alive. Have faith that better things are at hand for you, for the world. Never doubt it! Do not waste a moment in regret, discouragement, or resignation to an evil lot. Instead, envision this as a planet of pleasantness and peace. Devote every moment to expecting, praying for, working for, and discovering new blessings in life.

As you strive to establish and maintain right attitudes—spiritually, mentally, and emotionally—as well as right reactions to all that is happening in these dramatic times, you will truly become a powerful "weapon" for world peace.

CHAPTER 12

Prosperous Thinking for Health

One of the greatest blessings of life is health. Without it, nothing else matters very much. With good health, every other blessing is greatly enhanced. The more I learn about people and their various problems, the more I become aware of how strongly one's thought affects one's health.

For instance, many people are in poor health because of business worries and financial problems. A certain businessman enjoyed good health for a number of years; then he began to meet with financial setbacks in his business. He developed gastric ulcers that later were found to be malignant. Several operations have been necessary. He is now in the process of complete recovery, which his doctors are sure is possible. His wife recently reflected that every time this man has a financial setback he has to go back to bed, but every time he receives good news about his financial affairs, his spirit soars and he enjoys a much more normal physical condition.

Prosperous attitudes *can* enhance your health. To begin with, prosperous thinking is basically victorious, harmonious, uplifted thinking. A prosperous thinker dares to dwell on expanded ideas, visions, and expectations of good. A prosperous thinker knows how to free himself of hostilities, resentments, criticisms, and irritated emotions. A prosperous thinker aims for a normal, balanced attitude toward life which includes the "will to win." Such an attitude is the opposite of depression, discouragement, hostility, defeat, and other similar negative emotions that cause ill health.

A saleswoman had had a lingering cold for more than a year. Come summer or winter, the cold held on. She was beginning to wonder if she did not have something more serious than the "common cold." Her physician assured her, however, that he could find no organic cause for the cold's long duration.

When she visited a counselor, it was pointed out to her that physical irritation usually has a foundation of mental and emotional irritation, since the mind so strongly governs the body. The saleswoman then related how she had had a fine job, one she liked very much. Suddenly, without warning, her employer had transferred her to another department. She found the work there distasteful, even irritating. There was also great inharmony in that department among the various employees. This she also found irritating and distasteful. But she was afraid to protest the transfer because she feared losing her job. It was after this situation had arisen that her cold developed and persisted.

The counselor suggested that she begin working within her own thinking to overcome her feelings of hopelessness, discouragement, fear, and irritation about the situation. She was advised to adopt a victorious, winning attitude by daily affirming: *"Divine love and wisdom go before me, making easy and successful my way in this situation. The divine solution quickly and easily appears, I am now guided, healed, prospered, and blessed in all my ways."*

As the saleswoman began to fill her mind with these victorious ideas, she gained a sense of peace she had not had about her job during the past year. Just when she felt almost ready emotionally to approach her employer and discuss her job dissatisfaction, an interesting thing happened: a notice was placed on the bulletin board, stating that employees desiring transfers could see the manager, as he was considering making a number of changes! There was nothing now to stop this woman from declaring her desires, which were granted. As her inner feelings had changed and become harmonized her cold had slowly dissolved, and finally disappeared completely.

Where there is a condition of ill health, almost inevitably the one who is suffering has been subject to inharmony of mind, body, or affairs, and has not known how to adopt victorious, winning attitudes that could turn the tide of events. Prosperous thinking, expressing as harmonious thinking, helps produce harmony of body, as well as harmony in finances, in one's relationships, and in environments.

The power of thought to change the state of one's mind, body, and affairs is not a new teaching or theory. The ancient Babylonians were experts in the use of psychosomatics. It is believed that Abraham, who resided in the Babylonian city of Ur, learned of their use of this science and brought it to the Jews, who used it down through the centuries. In any event, the writers of the Bible seemed to understand that disease is caused by wrong thought and feeling. The first healing recorded in the Bible was in the time of Abraham: King Abimelech was healed after repenting for his wrong thoughts and actions regarding Abraham's wife. (It is interesting to realize that one definition of the word *repent* is "to change one's mind.")

Moses' sister Miriam contracted leprosy, after criticizing Moses for having married into another race. She was healed only as a result of Moses' prayer.

In another Old Testament instance, King Asa of Judah "was diseased in his feet." The Bible records that "his disease was exceeding great: yet in his disease he sought not to Jehovah, but to the physicians." Apparently he did not believe in spiritual healing, so he did not seek it. Accordingly he was not healed; "Asa slept with his fathers."

Elisha and Elijah both healed through mental and spiritual methods, as did Jesus, Paul, and many of the early Christians.

Truly, the body is the instrument of the mind. A businessman with a heart condition of long standing proved this. He was healed completely after he dared to adopt, deliberately and definitely, a pattern of prosperous, victorious thinking. I personally watched this man change from a defeated, unhappy, pale, thin individual into a man who was happy, confident, victorious, and in complete control of his world. New health, greater prosperity, and new family happiness resulted after he began to change his thinking. He accomplished this by affirming, *"There is good for me; I ought to have it, and I claim it now."*

Another businessman, who achieved wealth and total financial independence during the last decade, recently stated that these blessings had appeared (after long years of failure) when he, too, had deliberately changed his thought pattern from failure to success. The daily affirmation that helped him was: *"God is good. As His divine image and likeness, I am good. Everything that comes into my life is good, and I am going to have only the good. Health, wealth, and happiness are my divine right, and I claim and experience them now."*

A merchant, learning of the power of thought for health, took his wife to a lecture on prosperous thinking. For twelve years she had had a chronic gall-bladder condition, which was very painful most of the time. For over a year she had also had bursitis, which was growing progressively more painful, too. This man and his wife had done everything they knew to effect a healing. The finest medical treatment had not relieved the pain, nor had their prayers or those of friends.

The woman was beginning to feel she could not go on trying to live a normal life when she was in so much pain. Then, after hearing just one lecture on the power of thinking prosperously and victoriously, she realized that she could be healed. For the first time in months, both she and her husband felt uplifted and inspired; they began to image her complete healing, as well as success in every phase of their lives. The old hopelessness and discouragement dissolved as they affirmed: *"The spirit of success is now working with us. We are in all ways guided, healed, prospered, and blessed."*

As they began to change their thinking and their expectations in this simple way, an amazing thing happened: Within one week from the time they heard the lecture on the power of prosperous thinking and began daily affirming health and success, the woman's gall-bladder condition disappeared and the pain of the bursitis was completely dissolved, too. That was many months ago. She has continued in good health, and her husband has recently launched several new business ventures with great success. They continue to establish prosperous, victorious thought patterns by daily affirming health, wealth, and happiness.

A businesswoman broke her arm; though it mended nicely it was still filled with stiffness and pain a number of months later. She was unable to drive her car, which she needed in order to conduct her business affairs. She was quite discouraged about her health and her financial affairs, when she learned that a visiting speaker was scheduled to give a series of lectures in her town on the power of prosperous thinking. Determined to hear these lectures, she hired someone to drive her to the first one.

During the next week, as she reflected upon the power of successful, uplifted, victorious thinking, she began to realize that she could be completely whole and well again. This realization gave her new hope and an expectancy of good. She began daily affirming: "*I am the radiant child of God. My mind, body, and affairs now manifest His radiant perfection.*"

She knew that she should act upon her faith. One morning she decided. "I will no longer be in bondage to stiffness and pain. The doctor has said there is nothing physically wrong with my arm. It is healed. I now claim that complete healing." For the first time in months, she got into her car and drove about the city, conducting her business affairs. Instead of hurting her arm, the driving seemed to help relieve the stiffness and pain. By the time of the next lecture, a week later, all pain and stiffness had disappeared. She drove to that lecture and to other subsequent meetings alone, with no ill effects. Her arm was completely healed after she changed her thinking and dared to act upon her changed attitudes. Such is the power of prosperous thinking!

The great philosophers and sages of all times have tried to point out that man's health is controlled by his attitudes toward himself and others. Hippocrates, greatest of the Greek physicians, wrote around 400 B.C.: "Men ought to know that from the brain and from the brain only arise our pleasures, laughters, and jests, as well as our sorrows, pains, griefs, and fears." Plato declared, "If the head and body are to be well, you must begin by curing the soul." The Psalmist warned of the power of negative thinking:

"Cease from anger, and forsake wrath: fret not thyself, *it tendeth* only to evil-doing."

And Solomon surely realized the power of thought on one's life when he said:

"A glad heart maketh a cheerful countenance; but by sorrow of heart the spirit is broken."

As for the power of words to heal, he advised:

"Pleasant words are *as* a honeycomb, sweet to the soul, and health to the bones."

"The light of the eyes rejoiceth the heart; *and* good tidings make the bones fat."

Perhaps Solomon's greatest psychosomatic advice was this:

"A cheerful heart is a good medicine; but a broken spirit drieth up the bones."

A spirit that is "broken," discouraged, or subject to inharmonious conditions usually suffers a physical reaction. An understanding of the power of thought and feeling on one's health is needed in all walks of life. None of us is completely free of unhealthy emotions all the time. When weakness or sickness appears in the body, we need to know how to treat ourselves mentally as well as physically.

A clergyman had been in pain for several days, though his physician had prescribed medicine to ease the pain. When the prescription did not ease the pain, he telephoned friends who believed in the power of affirmative thought and prayer, requesting that they pray with him for healing. They suggested that he go to bed, relax as much as possible, and quietly affirm, *"I rest and relax in the love of God, and I am healed."* The next morning he telephoned his friends to tell them that he was feeling better but that the pain still persisted. They invited him to visit with them that morning, so that together they might look for the mental and emotional cause of the pain, while affirming complete healing. A brief conversation revealed that the young minister had been upset for a number of days. He had been in charge of certain phases of work in his church that were now being given to another minister; he was being transferred elsewhere. He secretly felt that an injustice had been done him, though he had not mentioned his feelings to anyone. To clear up his feeling of disturbance and injustice, he affirmed with his friends, *"God's love is doing its perfect work in this situation for the highest good of all concerned."* Soon he felt relieved and went home. He telephoned later to report that, at last, the pain was completely gone, and that he would continue affirming divine love and justice.

Then an interesting thing happened: At the ministers' conference it was announced that several scholarships were available for ministers who wished to do graduate study to fill certain specialized positions that were being created in his denomination. He was interested in this new field of work, applied for one of the scholarships, qualified, and was accepted. Within a short time, he entered a well-known seminary to do his graduate work. While there, he met the girl he later married.

Not only are victorious, uplifting attitudes and words helpful in effecting a healing: they are necessary to help *maintain* good health. A well-known doctor stated several years ago, "Griping can make you sick." I once knew a secretary who proved this. Negative thinking had become a habit with her, and she reacted to everything with unpleasant comments: the weather, the world in general, the man for whom she worked, her mother-in-law, other relatives, her neighbors. She constantly dwelt on unpleasant topics such as crime, disease, delinquency, war, and every other evil appearance or report that came to her attention.

She also complained about how bad she felt, though she spent hundreds of dollars on medical treatments, drugs, medicines of various types, chiropractic treatments, and so forth. Her many aches and pains continued to plague her, and she continued to "gripe" about them and everything else.

The result was that she had few friends. Her boss refused to give her a raise, though she had worked for him faithfully for a number of years. Her husband spent a great deal of time away from home; her mother-in-law and her neighbors constantly gave her a "hard time," to her way of thinking.

This woman heard about the technique of affirmative thought and prayer as a solution for her many problems. But she scoffed at this, declaring that it was too simple to be effective. She continued to think and speak negatively, and of course she continued to reap a harvest of unpleasant results.

Quite in contrast, a businessman once taught his wife a simple method for maintaining good health after she had experienced a serious operation. It had been predicted that in spite of the success of the operation, in all probability she would live not more than three months. However, her husband realized the effect of attitudes and words on the body, so he did not accept the three-month diagnosis as final. When his wife returned home, he reminded her that the body is the instrument of the mind. He said: "You've heard the three-month diagnosis. You can accept it and die, or you can reject it and live. But if you want to live you must do two things. First, you must stop talking about your operation and hospital experience; that only multiplies the condition. It is over; forget it. Second, you must think about life, affirm life, and expect to live. You can enjoy new health by affirming daily, *'Let divine health manifest in me now!'*"

She began using these simple words, and it became a subconscious habit to affirm them many times every day. When friends, neighbors, or business associates came to call, her husband always stated: "We are not discussing her operation or hospital experience. That is all over. She is now enjoying good health and expects to continue in good health." That was almost twenty-five years ago, and the woman has enjoyed good health all these years.

James Allen might have been summarizing the power of thought for health or lack of it when he wrote: "Disease and health, like circumstances, are rooted in thought. Sickly thoughts will express themselves through a sickly body. . . .

Strong, pure, and happy thoughts build up the body in vigor and grace.... If you would protect your body, guard your mind. If you would renew your body, beautify your mind."

Remind yourself often that your thoughts, feelings, and words strongly affect your health. Think and speak in terms of unlimited good for yourself and others. Your own body as well as your life and affairs will respond to your uplifted words. For your over-all success declare: "*Health, wealth, and happiness are mine by divine right. I claim them now.*" Specifically for health, affirm: "*I give thanks that I am the ever-renewing, ever-unfolding expression of infinite life, health, and energy. I am alive, alert, awake, joyous, and enthusiastic. Divine health now manifests in me.*"

CHAPTER 13

Controlled Living

One cold day, with our arms full of parcels, my young son and I waited impatiently to cross a busy street. On the other side, the warmth and comfort of our parked car awaited us. We had shopped in a suburban section of our city in which traffic signals had not yet been installed, and we had to wait until the lanes were free of traffic before we could make our crossing. As we stood there watching the heavy traffic and waiting to cross, I silently reproached myself for not shopping elsewhere. I thought about the convenience of zoned areas in which the red and green traffic signals aided both driver and pedestrian.

It later occurred to me that I had experienced a parallel for daily living. All of us may find ourselves in unzoned areas of living at times. We may stand on the curbing with our objective in view and yet seem unable to reach it. Inharmony, lack in mind, body, and affairs may arrest our attention and take command. And we may wait helplessly for these conditions to pass so that we can proceed toward our goal.

However, when one anxious situation passes and we are about to take a step forward, another may come rushing from a different direction, causing us to withdraw meekly again.

What is the real difficulty? What is the true obstacle overpowering us and hindering our progress and happiness? Is it some outside force, as we usually claim? Or does the trouble lie within ourselves? Why was I detained by the flowing traffic that cold day? Was it the fault of the persons driving by? Not at all; they were observing the rules of good driving and traveling toward their destinations unhampered by traffic signals. However, I was hindered from reaching my destination by the very factor aiding them.

This experience convinced me that all of us need to get into the zoned areas of living, where we will be directed toward our highest good. A zoned area is one that is enclosed by signals or otherwise made distinct. In reality, each of us is the center of a vast zoned area; and we are encircled by the omnipresence, omnipotence, and omniscience of our Creator. But we have to acknowledge His presence, power, and intelligence and claim His benefits, or obey His signals, before we can reap accordingly. How do we claim this divine heritage of good? Paul stated that it was through our mental attitude and our habitual thoughts. And he spoke from experience when he said, "Be ye transformed by the renewing of your mind."

We renew our minds through positive thinking, which is the expression of faith, confidence, certainty, optimism, the expectancy of good. Why does the practice of positive thinking contain such great power? Because through positive thought we set in motion the powerful Christian principles that Jesus taught and practiced. He looked for and dwelt on the good in all persons and situations rather than wasting time and thought on lesser appearances. Such a practice renewed His mind, body, and affairs and wrought miracles of good for others. Once when Peter attempted to call His attention to a questionable situation Jesus answered him, "What *is that* to thee? follow thou me." Today, centuries later, His answer still applies for us, His modern disciples.

Perhaps you know persons who seem to have that "certain something," who are able to forge ahead and to overcome worry and defeat. If so, you have doubtless wondered about their source of power. You will discover that they act, either consciously or unconsciously, upon Jesus Christ's statement, "All authority hath been given unto me in heaven and on earth." Through this state of mind, this mental attitude they have claimed the promise and are using it.

God reaches us and fills us with His power through our minds. He may be revealed to us through the signal of "a still small voice" of conscience. He may come through an idea that flashes into our minds or through the words of a friend or from an article we read. He may be revealed to us through prayer and meditation or through wisdom gained in an outer experience. But His communication will always reach our minds before we assimilate it and put it to work.

Although we send out hundreds of thoughts each day, they can affect us only in two ways. Thoughts are either positive or negative. If they are positive thoughts, usually expressed in faith and optimism, they will draw more good through channels of peace, health, prosperity, and love to us. If they are negative thoughts, usually expressed in fear, doubt, or pessimism, they will draw more negation to us through channels of illness, poverty, inharmony, and disaster. Job learned of this universal law of cause and effect and believed the same theory. He was speaking from vivid self-knowledge when he said, "The thing which I fear cometh upon me." Jesus was aware of the mental as well as the physical and spiritual realms. He taught that as we give so shall we receive when He said, "Give, and it shall be given unto you; good measure, pressed down, shaken together, running over ... For with what measure ye mete it shall be measured to you again."

Since we can get into the zoned areas of living and transform our experiences through the renewal of our minds, what practical steps should we take?

Daily practice of prayer is the first step. Prayer calms our outer thoughts and awakens the presence and power of Spirit within us and all around us. It is through prayer that we are personally directed to our individual good. Our daily experience in prayer should be simple to be effective and should be geared to meet our individual needs. Prayer is the most effective method of renewal and transformation, because in prayer man associates with God and not with the problem. Thus, he releases the problem to God for solution. In so doing, he is relieved of tension and struggle and experiences peace and renewal. This process makes way for the answer, which is what he has hoped and prayed for.

Daily practice of praise is another step. It brings out the good in both us and the other fellow. It produces harmony and good will. Praise is basically the practice of dwelling on the good in the persons and situations we encounter and making the most of that good. This is a challenge that can prove very stimulating.

Some authorities say that most of us use only about ten percent of our mental power. We merely exist when we could be doing a lot of happy, fruitful living. We often resist and battle life instead of relaxing and letting it unfold for us.

Why do we miss so much of our good? Is it not because of fear? Fear lessens, while faith increases and develops our mental power, talents, and opportunities. Often we do not have the faith, the self-confidence to try something new, to reach out to new experiences and new persons. We become bogged down with thoughts of doubt, uncertainty, failure, pessimism, and other negative emotions. Then we close our minds to the blessings that are already ours. We are either potential saints or sinners, according to the daily thoughts we harbor. And we cannot hide our thoughts because our lives reflect them. However, we can change them if we so desire and reap rich benefits.

Not only can we change our attitudes and consequently our lives through daily use of prayer and praise, we can also experience unlimited good through the powerful combination of prayer and praise in high, positive thought and vision. For me, the simple but promising statement, "*I go to meet my good*," is a miracle worker. I find that as I enter every experience with the thought that my good awaits me and I am going to meet it, unexpected opportunities and blessings appear, and my good is ready to greet me on every hand. The very "windows of heaven" seem to hear my call and to open. And if at times the response is not immediate, I find that repeated use of the statement, even orally and with words spoken firmly and expectantly, can be the key that unlocks the storehouse to my good.

Was it not a star that led ordinary men to the Christ child almost twenty centuries ago? The Spirit of the Christ child dwells within each of us and all around us today. Jesus Christ gave us this assurance when He said, "Lo, I am with you always." And we can find Him by following the star of Spirit within our individual consciousness and acting on its guidance.

The angel Gabriel appeared to Mary before the birth of Jesus and said, "Hail, thou that art highly favored, the Lord *is* with thee." This message was also meant for you and me; and as we accept it and act on its promise, we shall find ourselves being led out of the darkness into the light.

CHAPTER 14

A Master Plan for Success

What do you want to achieve, accomplish, experience? There is a simple method that can help you attain the success you truly desire. It is the use of a master plan for success.

There is nothing new about the power of a master plan. People often use a master plan to fail. They plan for failure, and they get it. Invariably, those who succeed over a long period are those who planned for success, and got it.

As you read the biographies of great men, you find that a master plan was usually followed by them or by someone near them, interested in their success. Much of the phenomenal success of Franklin D. Roosevelt could be attributed to a master plan. Twenty years before he became President, a master plan for his success was drawn up, by a man named Louis Howe. Howe became so convinced of Roosevelt's potential as a great leader that he refused to become disturbed when Roosevelt became ill. Instead, Howe mapped out a timetable for the future success of his friend. Twenty years later, when Franklin D. Roosevelt became President, Louis Howe had the satisfaction of witnessing an achievement for which he had been planning for twenty years.

Perhaps you are thinking, "Yes, but it was easier for Roosevelt to achieve his goals, because he had wealth and influence to aid him."

The master-plan idea works, regardless of any other conditions or circumstances. If you can conceive what you wish to accomplish within the next few years, work out a timetable for your success, and then just hold to that expectation, quietly working toward it. Your master plan will draw to you whatever else is needed to make your life as you wish it. Such is the magnetic power of the master plan!

Adolf Hitler used the master-plan idea destructively. He was unknown in the early 1920's. He had no money, no friends, no influence, and he was not trained for any specific work. But he did have a master plan which he outlined while in jail. In his book "Mein Kampf" he outlined his master plan. A recent biographer has said that World War II might have been avoided had the proper authorities taken Hitler's master plan seriously. Because he was an unknown, with only a jail record and some fantastic ideas, few believed him. But his master plan worked anyway, to the destruction of millions of people.

One of the great men of modern times who had a master plan for success was Winston Churchill. Early in his career he wanted to get into public life, but he was unknown to the public. He succeeded in getting some of the English newspapers to allow him to write for them, about the Cuban campaign, from India, and from various trouble spots around the world. His vivid newspaper accounts attracted a large following, and he became known to the British people. Then he began to run for various political offices. Every time he was defeated for an office, he would run for a more important one.

One biographer has said that the most mystifying aspect of the elections was Churchill's attitude when he lost: his manner was no different from that of the winner! After one defeat,

Churchill turned to the winner and said, "I don't think the world has heard the last of either of us." This remark, coming from a man who had just lost an election, confused the winner so much that he rushed out to recheck the election returns, to be sure that be had really won. Robert Lewis Taylor has written in his biography of Churchill, "He was a master planner."

Another modern leader whose career indicates a knowledge of the master-plan idea is President Charles de Gaulle of France. After World War II, he quietly retired to his country place, and it was generally assumed that his public life was over. One biographer has said that during that quiet period, lasting for twelve years, General de Gaulle spent a great deal of time in "study and meditation." He was studying his country's situation and meditating upon its return to greatness. It is little wonder that he became the one to lead France back to power.

There is nothing new about the master-plan idea. Some of the great men of the Bible succeeded in the face of great obstacles, through following their master plans. Perhaps one of the most outstanding examples is Joshua, one of the twelve spies Moses sent into the Promised Land. Joshua returned and described the land as rich. He brought back a great staff heavy with grapes to prove it. He stated his faith in the Hebrews' ability to go into the Promised Land immediately and possess it. But ten of the twelve spies gave negative reports, and Moses decided to wait.

The result was that the Children of Israel remained on the border of the Promised Land for forty years. During that time, Joshua served Moses in many ways. He quietly bided his time, keeping the vision of the Promised Land firmly in mind. He apparently had a detailed plan in mind for taking the land, because when he became the leader of the Hebrew people, he immediately informed them that they would pass over the Jordan into the Promised Land in just three days—and they did!

Fix your master plan in your mind, and keep thinking about it secretly. Then when the way begins to open for you to achieve results, you can do so very quickly. The longer your good is in coming, the greater it will be when it arrives!

A certain man is now much in the news as a candidate for governor of his State, and a presidential candidate. Several years ago, a stockbroker said to me: "Keep your eyes on that man. We will be hearing about him in the future, because he knows the power of the master plan."

Years before this man became president of his company, he had quietly worked out a master plan for its success. The day he became president, he took that plan out of his desk drawer and began executing it. Within a short time, his company was no longer a mediocre corporation. Its sales record during recent years has drawn national attention. This man has proved that it pays to have a master plan. He is still proving it, as he launches forth into new fields of endeavor.

I once met a woman who planned her way to success. Twenty years ago, she had nothing except hundreds of acres of pasture land, which were considered to be of little value. This land was located about a mile from the nearest highway and five miles from the nearest town. But this woman had a dream: she held in her mind the vision that one day her pasture land would become one of the most beautiful suburban shopping centers in the country.

In a few years, the nearby military base was enlarged. A four-lane highway was built, and it bordered on this woman's pasture land. Immediately realtors began making offers to purchase the land. But she did not want to sell it—she wanted to develop it.

She refused all offers and held on to her dream, though for financial reasons it seemed wise to sell.

Months went by, and then one day she noticed a contractor with his men and equipment working on property adjoining hers. She explained her dream to the contractor; he assured her that her dream could materialize, and that he would help. He suggested formation of a corporation in which she would furnish the land, and he would furnish equipment and men, and do the contracting and building. He explained that he had a wealthy friend who would provide financial backing and become the necessary third party in the corporation.

Today, the woman is president of that corporation, which owns a housing development, an apartment development, and a colonial-style shopping center—one of the most beautiful in the country. She had a plan, a vision. She dared to hold to her plan, and now she has all that she dared to envision, and more!

When you gain the vision of your master plan, refuse all offers of compromise or halfway success; quietly wait for the right situation to present itself before putting your plan into action. If you compromise once, you will have to keep on compromising, and the result will not be one of satisfying success.

Also, keep quiet about your master plan. Don't try to get somebody else's approval of it. Don't try to convince anyone else that you are right. The doubts of others can dissipate your dream. If you keep quiet about your dreams and keep believing in them, the same Power that gave you those dreams will give you the opportunities and all that is necessary for making them come true—at the right time, under the right circumstances.

A businessman had been in financial difficulties for some time. He heard about the master-plan idea, and he devised a master plan for his business that covered a five-year period. For months and months, he worked on this master plan, but nothing happened. Finally, through conversation with a friend who had introduced him to the master-plan idea, he realized why his plan was not working: He was trying to convince his wife and his mother-in-law that at last he was going to become a success. They kept doubting this, and their critical attitudes were neutralizing everything he was trying to do.

He saw that it was not necessary for him to convince them of his planned success. Instead, as he quietly invoked his master plan, saying nothing, the successful results did their own convincing.

A friend who has become financially independent through his stock-market transactions in recent years states that one of the reasons for his success is that he never discusses his business affairs with anyone. He affirms guidance in his financial affairs, quietly follows whatever leadings come, and says nothing. Early in the course of his transactions, he lost $20,000. If he had mentioned it to his family, they would have urged him not to invest anything more—and they would have missed out on the fortune that he has since made on the stock market. "In quietness and in confidence shall be your strength."

A Pulitzer prize winner once gave this worthwhile advice: "When you have laid out a course of action for yourself, calculate the risks ahead and then go through with your course of action, no matter what is going on. Don't be flurried and don't get panicky. The man who stops to take counsel of his fears is the man who is lost. Safety and success lie ahead and nowhere else.

No one ever reaches them if he stops to worry about the unseen."

A lawyer began invoking the master-plan idea early in his career. He and his father shared two small law offices with their secretaries. These offices were located in an old building on the town square, amid much noise. One day the son dictated to his secretary a master plan for the firm's growth during the next five years.

He stated in detail his desires for the firm. He wanted to expand from a two-man law firm to a five-man or six-man firm, which would include a trial lawyer, a tax specialist, and a junior member to handle much of the detail work. He wanted each lawyer to have his own secretary, with a principal secretary who would be in charge of the others. He desired new, comfortable, air-conditioned offices. He set down the increase in income he desired for the firm, year by year, over the five-year period. At the time he dictated all these expectations, it seemed an impossible dream. In the following months he often reviewed his master plan.

Soon a third man, talented as a trial lawyer, came into the firm. A whole floor of new offices was offered the firm in a bank building. These new offices included a conference room and a kitchen, in addition to ample space for each attorney and secretary. A fourth lawyer who had just finished law school was employed. He became the junior member and relieved the other lawyers of many detailed assignments. The income of the firm mounted. Later, a tax specialist joined the firm. Today that law firm is one of the most prominent in the State. The man who devised and invoked the master plan for its success recently served as president of an international service organization. Such is the power of the master plan: not only does it work in ways we can foresee and plan for, it also provides us with blessings beyond what we can envision.

Success comes when you move unerringly forward, rejecting all that tends to distract you from your master plan. You are well equipped to live life fully and to master life in its every phase, if you dare to work out a master plan of your desires (in as much detail as possible) for the next few years and then dwell quietly upon them. It is good to list dates by which you wish certain desires fulfilled.

When we become definite and positive in our thinking, even as regards the time element, it is as though we tap a special power in the universe which rushes forth to arrange events, causing our stipulated results to appear by the specified dates. Often we let our desired good slip by us because we do not list our desires and the dates by which we wish them to appear as visible, satisfying results in our lives.

I once met a fine young man who was already on the way to becoming a millionaire. He stated that his success began at the age of eighteen, when he dared to work out a twelve-year plan for his success. He wanted to be financially independent at the age of thirty. After working out his master plan, it not only began to work but gained momentum, so that his desires had been completely fulfilled several years before his thirtieth birthday.

Never underestimate the power of the master plan. It is scientific, it is practical, it is businesslike, and it works! Even though your master plan may not produce immediate results, if you will develop it and keep thinking about it, you will feed it with your mind power and with your faith. Eventually all obstacles will be dissolved and you will enter your "promised land."

Here is a final point to remember: Success has a way of coming in a hurry after you have endured a "long haul" of plodding along slowly.

As you quietly persist toward your goal, prepare yourself for quick, exciting, success-filled results. Have your plans made as to what you will do when success arrives, because just when it may seem least likely, the tide can turn for you. Then it will be necessary for you to take a deep breath, and proceed to accept your abundance of good.

As fulfillment comes, you must not let it unbalance you. Be alert and ready to accept it; otherwise, it may slip away, leaving you to begin all over again. If you have a master plan, it will be easier for you to accept your success and maintain it.

To paraphrase the words of Paul: "Forget the things that are behind. Press forward toward your goal!" Now, as you work out your master plan for success, affirm: *"Father, let the master plan of my life now reveal itself to me. Let the master plan of my life now begin working for me. I give thanks for my master plan of success. I give thanks for the perfect results of that master plan. With God's help I now plan my way to success; with God's help I now begin to experience the results of my master plan."*

www.ingramcontent.com/pod-product-compliance
Lightning Source LLC
Chambersburg PA
CBHW072200070526
44585CB00015B/1229